More praise for *Leading the Transformation*

"It's long past the time when executives who are looking for better performance from software development can expect an "Agile transformation" to solve their problems. Today's wise executive will know enough about the underlying principles of software systems to ask the right questions and make sure that their organization is solving the right problems. That's where this book comes in—it contains just enough theory to inform executives about critical issues and just enough detail to clarify what's important and why."

—Mary Poppendieck, author of *The Lean Mindset*
and the Lean Software Development series

"*Leading the Transformation* is a critical asset for any leadership in a large development environment seeking to transform the organization from the swamp of restriction to the freeway of efficient delivery. The book provides real-life data and solid advice for any leader embarking on or in the middle of an enterprise delivery transformation."

—Lance Sleeper, Senior Manager of
Operations, American Airlines

"Before you undertake a major change in your development process, you want to learn from people who have gone before you. Gary and Tommy draw on their experience to prepare you for how to plan and what to expect as you roll out Agile/DevOps methodology in your enterprise. Reading this book, I learnt valuable lessons on planning a scaled-out Agile transformation and what signposts to look for along the way as we embarked on the transformation journey at Cisco."

—Vinod Peris, VP Engineering, Routing & Optical, Cisco

‖‖‖LEADING
THE TRANSFORMATION

LEADING
THE TRANSFORMATION

Applying Agile and DevOps Principles at Scale

Gary Gruver and Tommy Mouser

Foreword by Gene Kim

IT Revolution
Portland, OR

IT Revolution
Portland, OR
info@itrevolution.net

For quantity purchases by corporations, associations, and others,
please contact the publisher at orders@itrevolution.net.

Cover, illustrations, and interior design by
Brian David Smith and Mammoth Collective.

To our amazing wives, Carolyn and Debbie

CONTENTS

Foreword by Gene Kim   11

Chapter 1   Understanding the Transformation   13

Chapter 2   Challenges with Scaling Agile Teams   20

Chapter 3   Business Objectives and Crucial First Steps   26

Chapter 4   Enterprise-Level Continuous Improvement   33

Chapter 5   Agile Enterprise Planning   38

Chapter 6   Business Objectives Specific to Scaling DevOps   50

Chapter 7   Creating a Culture of Trunk Development   55

Chapter 8   Ensuring a Solid Foundation   61

Chapter 9   Continuous Delivery   72

Chapter 10   Designing the Deployment Pipeline   82

Chapter 11   Improving Stability Over Time   91

Chapter 12   Getting Started   101

Further Reading   105

Acknowledgements   107

FOREWORD

I first came across Gary and Tommy's amazing work transforming how HP developed firmware code for the entire HP LaserJet Enterprise product line when Jez Humble told me about it. It was an astounding story of Continuous Delivery and DevOps for many reasons. Their story of being able to increase the development of new customer functionality by two to three times was a breathtaking leap in developer productivity. But that this success story was for embedded firmware for printers made it almost defy belief.

I believe that the HP LaserJet case study is important because it shows how Continuous Delivery and DevOps principles transcend all technology and that DevOps isn't just for open source software. Instead, it should be equally applicable for complex enterprises systems, systems of record—even those 30-plus-year-old COBOL applications that run on mainframes.

This theory was put to the test and proven when Gary became VP of QE, Release, and Operations at Macys.com. For three years, he helped contribute to the transformation that went from doing thousands of manual tests every ten days to thousands of automated tests being run daily, increasing the ability to have all applications closer to a deployable state.

In fifteen years, I suspect that everything Gary and Tommy have done for large, complex organizations will be common knowledge for technology executives. However, in the meantime, the challenges of how large, complex organizations adopt DevOps will create incredible competitive advantage, and I hope this book becomes a catalyst for making that knowledge more commonplace.

—Gene Kim
Portland, Oregon
April 2015

CHAPTER 1
UNDERSTANDING THE TRANSFORMATION

There are large organizations in the industry using leading-edge techniques such as Agile and DevOps to develop software faster and more efficiently than anyone ever thought possible. These are typically companies that learned how to architect and develop software well while they were still relatively small. They then grew large quickly because of these breakthrough capabilities. Think Google, Amazon, and Facebook.

Currently, however, the majority of software is not developed by leading-edge groups like these, but by more traditional organizations using less efficient approaches. This book is written to help leaders of these traditional organizations understand how to successfully transform their development and delivery processes.

Improving the effectiveness of software development in traditional organizations is essential because software is a key way businesses now compete across a broad range of industries. Mechanical engineers that designed and built cars led the automobile industry. Then, through no fault of their own, they found that computers had infiltrated their product and become a larger part of the value they provide their customers. Now, instead of the salesman showing off the car engine, they start with a screen for the entertainment and control system—all based on software. Financial institutions that used to depend on traders working the floor and brokers forging customer relationships are finding that software for managing trades and interacting with their customers is helping them stay competitive. Retail has gone from building, stocking, and managing stores to creating software that provides a common customer experience across stores, websites, and mobile devices and that manages inventory more efficiently across all these channels.

No industry is immune from the far-reaching changes based on the increasing influence of software. Jeff Immelt, CEO of General Electric, warns, "In an industrial company, avoid [gaining mastery of] software at your peril. We are paranoid because a software company could someday disintermediate GE. I'm going back to school on big data and software."

While it is clear that software is becoming a more and more important aspect of how these companies need to compete, most large, traditional organizations are struggling to deliver. They can't respond to changes in the marketplace fast enough, and the businesses are getting frustrated. These companies are typically struggling with lots of hard-to-change, tightly coupled legacy software that requires them to coordinate development, qualification, and deployment efforts across hundreds to thousands of engineers, making frequent deliveries impossible. The deliveries they do provide require lots of brute-force manual effort that is frustrating and burning out their teams.

The net result is that most large, traditional organizations are finding it more and more difficult to compete in the marketplace and deliver the software innovations that their businesses require. Their current software delivery approaches are constraining their businesses and limiting their ability to compete.

Because their current approaches don't work, many larger organizations are looking to leverage the successes that smaller businesses have seen using Agile methodologies. They bring in Agile coaches and start forming Agile teams to apply Agile principles at the team level. The problem with this approach is that in small organizations, a couple of small Agile teams can organize to support the business. In large, traditional organizations, however, most of the time individual teams can't independently deliver value to the customer because it requires integrating work across hundreds of developers and addressing all the inefficiencies of coordinating this work. These are issues that the individual teams can't and won't solve on their own. This is why the executives need to lead the transformation. They are uniquely positioned to lead the all-important cultural changes and muster the resources to make the necessary organization-wide technical changes.

In this book we, the authors, will provide a fundamentally different approach for transforming the software development processes in large, traditional organizations by addressing the organization-wide issues that you, the executives, are uniquely positioned to handle. While most Agile implementations start with a focus on applying Agile principles at the team level, the approach presented in this book focuses on applying the basic principles of Agile and DevOps across the organization. It is based on what we, as executives leading complex transitions in large, traditional organizations, have found to be most effective for delivering solid business results.

Many specifics referenced in this book are leveraged from a case study of transformation at HP, detailed in *A Practical Approach to Large-Scale Agile Development*, by Gary Gruver, Mike Young, and Pat Fulghum.

This case study includes the following dramatic results:

» Development costs reduced from ~$100M to ~$55M

» 140% increase in the number of products being supported

» Increased capacity for innovation from 5% to 40%

The organization at HP achieved these results through applying DevOps and Agile principles at scale. Our focus was on applying the principles at the executive staff level, and we left the teams with as much flexibility in operational choices as possible. There were some groups that applied all the team-level Agile principles and some that chose to operate with more traditional methods.

What we found in the end is that there were not dramatic differences in the teams' productivity based on the methods they used. There were, though, dramatic improvements in the overall productivity of the entire organization. This lead to our conclusion that *how teams come together to deliver value* in large organizations is the first-order effect, while *how individual teams work* was a second-order effect. Therefore, this book will primarily focus on how to transform the way the teams come together to provide value to the business by integrating all their changes early and often in an operation-like environment. This is one of the most important steps in improving the effectiveness of large organizations, because it forces resolving conflicts between teams early before too much time and effort is wasted on code that won't work together in production. Then, when that part of the transformation is complete, the organization will have the right framework in place to continue improving and fine-tuning how the individual teams work with more traditional Agile methods at the team level.

Executives need to understand that applying Agile and DevOps principles at scale both differs significantly from typical Agile implementations and provides quicker time to value. To help executives understand why, they need to understand the challenges that large organizations experience with traditional approaches. In chapter 2 we will dissect the Waterfall Method, look at the Agile principles that answer Waterfall's shortcomings, and then uncover key challenges that result from using a more traditional Agile approach in the enterprise.

The first step executives need to understand about our approach is that it is paramount to begin with business objectives. You should never "do Agile or DevOps" just so you can say you did them. A large-scale transformation is too much work and turmoil just to be able to say you are "doing Agile." We believe that the key reason executives would be willing to take on this much change is that their current development processes are failing to meet the overarching needs of the business. Executives are in the best position to understand those failings and the needs of the business, so they are best suited to clarify the objectives of the transformation. In chapter 3, we will go into how executives begin to lead the transformation, using these objectives to communicate the vision, prioritize improvements, and show progress.

Once the business objectives have clarified the long-term goals of the transformation, executives then will use an enterprise-level continuous improvement process to engage the organization throughout the journey. Because it is so hard to measure process improvements with software, executives can't just manage the change by metrics like they would other parts of their business. They are going to have to engage with the organization to get a more qualitative understanding of what is working and what needs fixing next. This transformation can't be top-down, just like it can't be bottom-up.

The continuous improvement process is designed to engage the broader organization in setting objectives the team feels are important and achievable. Additionally, since a transformation of this size can take years and is going to be such a discovery process, it is designed to capture and respond to what everyone is learning along the way. The executives will use a combination of the business objectives and the continuous improvement process to lead the transformation and prioritize improvements based on what will provide the biggest benefit to the business. We will cover the continuous improvement process in more detail in chapter 4, including setting short-term objectives for each iteration, focusing on what everyone is learning, and identifying what is and isn't working to determine priorities for the next iteration.

In this book we will use the term *enterprise-level* to describe an organization with software development efforts that require 100 or more engineers to coordinate the development, qualification, and release of their code. It does not refer to a coordinated effort across an organization the size of HP, because that would just be too complex. The plan for transforming the organization should be kept as small as possible to reduce complexity. But if different applications in the enterprise have to be qualified together to ensure they work in production, then they should be included as part of the same enterprise-level transformation.

FIGURE 1

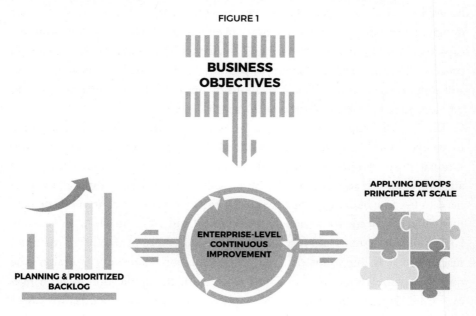

BUSINESS OBJECTIVES

PLANNING & PRIORITIZED BACKLOG

ENTERPRISE-LEVEL CONTINUOUS IMPROVEMENT

APPLYING DEVOPS PRINCIPLES AT SCALE

Once the business objectives and continuous improvement process are in place, executives can start changing development processes by applying Agile and DevOps principles at scale. This will require two big changes: applying Agile principles to the planning process and using DevOps to address the basic Agile principle of being able to economically release smaller batches of changes on a more frequent basis.

Executives need to understand that managing software and the planning process in the same way that they manage everything else in their organization is not the most effective approach. Software has a few characteristics that are different enough from everything else that it makes sense to take a different approach. First, each new software project is new and unique, so there is a higher degree of uncertainty in the planning. Second, the ability of organizations to predict the effectiveness of software changes is so poor that literally 50% of all software is never used or does not meet its business objectives.[1] Third, unlike any other asset in a business, if software is developed correctly it is much more flexible and cheaper to change in response to shifts in the market. If the planning process doesn't take these differences into account, executives are likely to make the classic mistake of locking in their most flexible asset to deliver features that will never be used or won't ever meet the business intent. Additionally, if executives don't design the planning process correctly, it can end up using a lot of the organization's capacity without providing much value. In chapter 5, we will cover how to design processes to minimize investments in planning and requirement breakdown but still support the critical business decisions by breaking the planning process into different time horizons and locking in capacity over time.

The DevOps approach of integrating working code across the organization in an operation-like environment is one of the biggest challenges for large, traditional organizations, but it provides the most significant improvements in aligning the work across teams. It also provides the real-time feedback engineers need to become better developers. For this to work well, the continuous deployment pipeline needs to be designed to quickly and efficiently localize issues in large, complex systems and organizations. It requires a large amount of test automation, so it is important that the test automation framework is designed to quickly localize issues and can easily evolve with the application as it changes over time. This is a big challenge for most organizations, so the executives need to make sure to start with achievable goals and then improve stability over time as the organization's capabilities improve. Teams can't and won't drive this level of change, so the executives need to understand these concepts in enough detail to lead the transformation and ensure their teams are on the right track. Therefore, we spend a lot of time on applying DevOps principles at scale in chapters 6–11.

Transforming development and delivery processes in a large, traditional organization requires a lot of technical changes that will require some work, but by far the biggest challenges are with changing the culture and how people work on a day-to-day basis.

What do these cultural shifts look like? Developers create a stable trunk in a production-like environment as job #1. Development and Operation teams use common tools and environments to align them on a common objective. The

1. Ronny Kohavi et al, "Online Experiments at Microsoft," Microsoft Research website, accessed April 1, 2015, http://research.microsoft.com/en-us/projects/thinkweek/expthinkweek2009public.pdf.

entire organization agrees that the definition of done at the release branch means that the feature is signed off, defects-free, and the test automation is ready in terms of test coverage and passing rates. The organization embraces the unique characteristics of software and designs a planning process that takes advantage of software's flexibility. These are big changes that will take time, but without the executives driving these cultural shifts, the technical investments will be of limited value.

From business objectives and continuous improvement to planning and DevOps, *Leading the Transformation* takes you through the step-by-step process of how to apply Agile and DevOps principles at scale. It is an innovative approach that promises markedly better business results with less up-front investment and organizational turmoil.

|||||| CHAPTER 2
CHALLENGES WITH SCALING AGILE TEAMS

Traditional implementations that focus on scaling small Agile teams across the organization are very different from applying Agile and DevOps principles at scale. Executives play a key role in communicating the advantages of the latter approach and in explaining how it differs from what is typically done in the industry. This chapter outlines the basic Agile principles for executives and highlights the limitations of the typical approach of scaling small teams across the organization. This information is vital to executives looking to avoid the struggles of traditional implementations and to capitalize on the business benefits of a successful transformation.

Waterfall Method vs. Agile

As many executives know, the Waterfall Method of development leverages project management principles used for managing many types of projects. It starts by gathering requirements and then planning all the work. Development begins after the planning, and then software is integrated for the final qualification and release. The goal of this approach is to structure the program such that you can determine the schedule, scope, and resources up front.

Large, complex software development projects, however, are fundamentally different than other types of projects, and traditional project management approaches are not well equipped to deal with these differences. Software development is such a discovery process that many of the assumptions made in the planning stage quickly become obsolete during development. Additionally, integration and qualification tends to uncover major issues late in the process, which results in frequent and costly schedule slips and/or working the teams to death.

The first step in leading the transformation is understanding that Agile principles are a response to the shortcomings of using traditional Waterfall project management approaches for software. They were proposed as a framework to address these unique software development challenges.

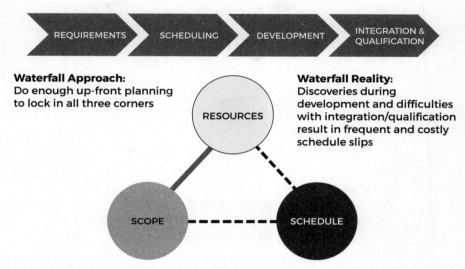

FIGURE 2: WATERFALL DEVELOPMENT MODEL

REQUIREMENTS SCHEDULING DEVELOPMENT INTEGRATION & QUALIFICATION

Waterfall Approach:
Do enough up-front planning to lock in all three corners

Waterfall Reality:
Discoveries during development and difficulties with integration/qualification result in frequent and costly schedule slips

RESOURCES

SCOPE

SCHEDULE

Instead of long phases of requirements, planning, development, and qualification, there are much smaller iterations where complete features are integrated and qualified on a regular basis. Additionally, the entire code base is kept stable so that the code can be released at the end of each iteration, if required. This fixes the schedule and resources while letting the scope absorb the program uncertainty. The features are all worked on in priority order, with the most valuable features being developed first. Agile practitioners have numerous examples where after delivering less than 50% of the original must-have features, the customer is happy with the product and no longer requesting more features.

Contrast this with the Waterfall Method, where there are no regular code drops. The qualification and integration process would not have started until all the must-have features were complete, taking much longer to deliver any value and creating features that may not have been necessary. While there are many other benefits to Agile, this highlights the key breakthrough for the business and as such is imperative for executives to understand when contemplating leading a large-scale Agile transformation.

Change Management Capacity

Transitioning to Agile is a very big effort for a large organization. There are technical and process changes required. Frequently, organizations focus on the

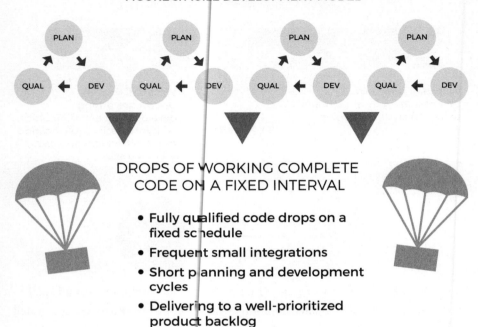

FIGURE 3: AGILE DEVELOPMENT MODEL

PLAN PLAN PLAN PLAN

QUAL ← DEV QUAL ← DEV QUAL ← DEV QUAL ← DEV

DROPS OF WORKING COMPLETE CODE ON A FIXED INTERVAL

- Fully qualified code drops on a fixed schedule
- Frequent small integrations
- Short planning and development cycles
- Delivering to a well-prioritized product backlog

technical solutions. While required, they represent a smaller portion of the effort. Most of the real challenges are in organizational change management and shifting the culture. Executives need to understand that the capacity of the organization to absorb change is the biggest constraint to rolling out these improvements. This means that the organizational change management capacity is the most precious resource, and it should be actively managed and used sparingly.

The approach to rolling out an enterprise-level Agile transition should focus on the business breakthroughs the Agile principles are intended to achieve while taking into consideration the capacity of an organization to change. This is where executives can add knowledge and expertise.

The Limitations of Traditional Agile Implementation: An Executive Perspective

What follows is an example of a large (1,000-developer) organization that tries to enable small Agile teams in the organization. The example is not real, but it is a snapshot of what is being done in the industry today.

The first step is to select a few pilot teams with eight to ten members who will start being "Agile." These teams will gain valuable experience and create some best practices. Once these teams have demonstrated the advantages of Agile, they create a plan for how it should be done for this organization. The plan will need to scale across the organization, so in the end there are going to be ~100 Agile teams. Agile coaches will be hired to get a few teams going, and then within a year, all the teams should be up and running. Throughout the year, each coach can probably ramp up about five teams; thus, this rollout could require in the range of 20 coaches. With a cost of $150/hour, this adds up to over $2M/year. When forming Agile teams, it is important to understand that you want teams that can own the whole feature end to end, so you need to pick members from the different component teams to form the prototype teams. This works fine with just a few teams, but when we start rolling this out organization-wide, we are going to need a complete reorganization. Once everyone is in teams creating effective workspaces for collaboration, moving everyone around will probably take another $1–2M.

The next step is making sure the teams have the right tool for documenting and tracking their Agile stories, which will probably run $1M or more. All of a sudden, we are up to over $5M for the transition. We better make sure we talk to the executives who can commit that level of resources. This will require a ROI justification to the CFO. So now we are committed to a big investment and a big return to the top-level executives. At this point, we have an implementation that engages and includes the engineers and the top-level executives. The management team in the middle, however, does not have a clear role except to provide their support and stay out of the way.

There are a number of problems with this whole approach. You are now $4–5M into a transition, and you still don't have a plan for having always-releasable code for the enterprise or an enterprise backlog. Teams may have a clear local definition of "done" in their dedicated environments and team backlogs, but at the enterprise level you have not changed the process for releasing code. Also, this approach has driven lots of organizational change that may be met with some resistance. We started with taking managers out of the process because they are a big part of the problem and don't understand how to coach Agile teams. Can you see why and how they might undermine this transformation? Next, we have a complete reorganization, which always tends to be a cause for concern and creates resistance to change. Add to that moves designed to get teams together in collaborative workspaces. You can see how this approach is going create a lot of turmoil and change while not fundamentally changing the frequency of providing code to the customers for feedback.

The other big challenge is getting the teams to buy in and support how they are going to approach the details of their day-to-day work. The first prototype teams are going to be successful because they had a lot of input in defining the team-level processes and have ownership of its success. The problem most organizations have is that once they have determined the "right" way for their teams to do Agile, they feel the next step is teaching everyone one else to do it that way. This approach of telling the teams how to do their day-to-day work feels like it is contrary to the good management practices that we learned early in our careers.

In most cases, for any problem there are at least three different approaches that will all achieve the same solution. On the one hand, if we were really smart managers, we could pick the best approach and tell the team how to do it. If, on the other hand, we let the team pick how to meet the objective, they are more likely to make their idea more successful than they would have made our idea. If we told them how to do it and it failed, it was clear that we didn't have a very good idea. If they got to pick the *how*, then they were much more likely to do whatever it took to make their idea successful. Just being managers or being part of the prototype team did not mean we were any more likely to pick the best idea.

Therefore, as leaders we feel it is important, wherever possible, to provide the framework with the objectives and let the team have as much design flexibility in defining how the work will get done. It provides them with more interesting work, and they take more ownership of the results. In addition, when the situation changes, those doing the work are likely to sense it and adapt more quickly than an executive would.

Summary

What we hope executives walk away with after reading this example is that most Agile implementations struggle to provide expected business results because they focus on rolling out Agile teams the "right" way instead of applying Agile principles at scale. This approach creates a lot of change management challenges in an organization without fundamentally addressing the basic Agile business principles of an enterprise backlog and always-releasable code. We believe our approach offers answers to a lot of these struggles. Having the executives and managers leading the transformation by setting the business objectives and running the continuous improvement process engages them in the transformation. Focusing on improving the organization-wide planning and delivery processes provides clarity on the business breakthroughs the basic Agile principles were intended to provide. Providing a framework for prioritizing and integrating work across the teams provides the basic processes for improving the effectiveness of large organizations while providing the teams with as much flexibility as possible in defining how they work on a day-to-day basis. What follows is a detailed account of how each step of the process builds on the next. What you end up with is a concrete plan to apply Agile principles at scale to help executives lead the transformation in their own businesses.

CHAPTER 3
BUSINESS OBJECTIVES AND CRUCIAL FIRST STEPS

BUSINESS OBJECTIVES

The reason these two Agile authors say "don't do Agile" is that we don't think you can ever be successful or get all the possible business improvements if your objective is simply to do Agile and be done. Agile is such a broad and evolving methodology that it can't ever be implemented completely. Someone in your organization can at any time Google "What is Agile development" and then argue for pair programing or Extreme Program or less planning, and you begin a never-ending journey to try all the latest ideas without any clear reason why. Additionally, Agile is about continuous improvement, so by definition you will never be done.

At HP we never set out to do Agile. Our focus was simply on improving productivity. The firmware organization had been the bottleneck for the LaserJet business for a couple of decades. In the few years before this transformation started, HP tried to spend its way out of the problem by hiring developers around the world, to no avail. Since throwing money at the problem didn't work, we needed to engineer a solution.

We set off on a multiyear journey to transform the way we did development with the business objective of freeing up capacity for innovation and ensuring that, after the transformation, firmware would not be the bottleneck for shipping new products. This clear objective really helped guide our journey and prioritize the work along the way. Based on this experience and others like it, we think the most important first step in any transformation is to develop a clear set of business objectives tuned to your specific organization to ensure you are well positioned to maximize the impact of the transformation on business results.

We see many companies that embark on a "do Agile" journey. They plan a big investment. They hire coaches to start training small Agile teams and plan a big organizational change. They go to conferences to benchmark how well they are "doing DevOps or Agile." They see and feel improvements, but the management teams struggle to show bottom-line business results to the CFO. Not having clear business objectives is a key source of the problem. If they started out by focusing on the business and just using DevOps ideas or implementing some Agile methods that would provide the biggest improvements, they would find it much easier to show bottom-line financial results. This worked at HP. When we started, firmware had been the bottleneck in the business for a couple of decades and we had no capacity for innovation. **At the end of a three-plus-year journey, adding a new product to our plans was not a major cost driver. We had dramatically reduced costs from $100M to $55M per year and increased our capacity for innovation by eight times.**

To be clear, achieving these results was a huge team effort. For example, it required us to move to a common hardware platform so that a single trunk of code could be applied to the entire product line up. Without the collaboration with our partners throughout the business we could not have achieved these results. Having a set of high-level business objectives that the entire organization is focused on is the only way to get this type of cross-organizational cooperation and partnership. These types of results will not happen when you "do Agile." It takes a laser-like focus on business objectives, a process for identifying inefficiencies in the current process, and implementing an ongoing, continuous improvement process.

Where to Start

Once you have a clear set of business objectives in place, the next step is determining where to start the transformation. You can't do everything at once and this is going to be a multiyear effort, so it is important to start where you will get the biggest benefits.

From our perspective, there are two options that make sense for determining where to start. The first is the activity-based accounting and cycle-time approach that we used at HP. You start with a clear understanding of how people are spending their time and the value the software is intended to provide to your business. This approach addresses the biggest cost and cycle-time drivers that are not key to your business objectives. The challenge with this approach is that sometimes it can be very time-consuming to get a good understanding of all the cost and cycle-time drivers.

The other approach is to focus on the areas that are typically the biggest sources of inefficiencies in most enterprise software development efforts: maintaining always-releasable code and your planning processes. Then apply DevOps and Agile principles to these areas. The beauty of software is that once you develop a new feature, the marginal cost of delivering that feature should be almost zero. This is not the case in most organizations that are either using Waterfall development methodologies or have focused their Agile implementations on scaling Agile teams. Neither do a good job of addressing the biggest organization-level inefficiencies like fixing the planning process or enabling easy, more frequent releases of new features. This approach starts with applying DevOps and Agile principles at scale to address these enterprise-level inefficiencies first.

Activity-Based Accounting and Cycle-Time Approach

At HP our clear business objectives of freeing up capacity for innovation and no longer being the bottleneck for the business meant we needed to dramatically improve productivity. Therefore, we started by understanding our cost and cycle-time drivers to identify waste in our development processes. We determined these by mapping our processes, thinking about our staffing, digging through our finances, and looking back at our projects under development. This is an important first step. Most people understand how they are spending money from a cost-accounting perspective. They have detailed processes for allocating costs out to products or projects. They don't have an activity-based accounting view of what is driving the costs. This step requires either a deep understanding of how people spend their time or a survey of the organization. Also keep in mind that while it does not have to be accurate to three significant digits, you do need to have a reasonably good feel for the cost and cycle-time drivers to prioritize your improvement ideas. The result of this analysis at HP is documented in figure 4a.

Once we were clear about our business objectives, cycle-times, and cost drivers, we were ready to start our improvement process. We focused on waste in the system, which we defined as anything driving time or cost that was not key to our business objectives. It was only at this point that we considered changing our development approach to align with some of the DevOps and Agile methods. We also wanted to make sure we were starting where we could show quick progress. There are lots of different starting points and an organization can only change so many things at once, so we wanted to make sure we began where we would get the biggest return on our investment. This would enable us to show progress as soon as possible and free up capacity for more improvements.

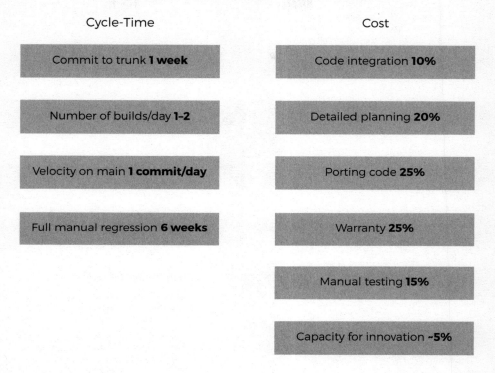

FIGURE 4A: CYCLE-TIME AND COST DRIVERS 2008

Cycle-Time	Cost
Commit to trunk **1 week**	Code integration **10%**
Number of builds/day **1-2**	Detailed planning **20%**
Velocity on main **1 commit/day**	Porting code **25%**
Full manual regression **6 weeks**	Warranty **25%**
	Manual testing **15%**
	Capacity for innovation **~5%**

Our build, integration, and testing process was driving both cost and cycle-times, so we figured that was a good place to start. When we looked in the DevOps and Agile toolbox, we picked continuous integration as one of our first objectives. We also realized we were spending a lot of effort doing detailed planning for development that never went as planned. We knew we had to do something different for planning, so the idea of iterations with short-term objectives felt like a great second improvement idea. We never did set off with the objective to transition from Waterfall to Agile development or implement DevOps. We never went in and justified to yet higher levels of management that we wanted to fund a big transformation. We just set in play a continuous improvement process where we would set objectives and review results each iteration. Additionally, we started focusing in on improving our build and integration process because this was where we thought we would get the best improvements in productivity.

This approach led us on a three-plus-year journey, one monthly iteration at a time, which ended up providing some pretty dramatic improvements. Over time

FIGURE 4B: CYCLE-TIME DRIVER IMPROVEMENTS

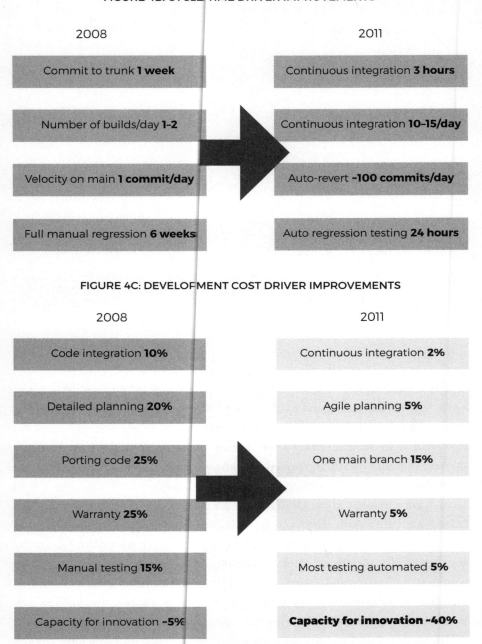

2008	2011
Commit to trunk **1 week**	Continuous integration **3 hours**
Number of builds/day **1–2**	Continuous integration **10–15/day**
Velocity on main **1 commit/day**	Auto-revert **~100 commits/day**
Full manual regression **6 weeks**	Auto regression testing **24 hours**

FIGURE 4C: DEVELOPMENT COST DRIVER IMPROVEMENTS

2008	2011
Code integration **10%**	Continuous integration **2%**
Detailed planning **20%**	Agile planning **5%**
Porting code **25%**	One main branch **15%**
Warranty **25%**	Warranty **5%**
Manual testing **15%**	Most testing automated **5%**
Capacity for innovation **~5%**	**Capacity for innovation ~40%**

2011 intentionally not = 100%. The difference was used for further process improvements.

we found more and more methods out of the DevOps and Agile toolbox that helped improve our productivity, and we chose to roll them out as part of our continuous improvement iteration process. There are several approaches from the toolbox that we had still not implemented at that point and some we intentionally chose not to implement because we felt the benefit was not worth the investment. That said, prioritizing methods based on business objectives that we felt would have the biggest impact on our cycle-time and cost drivers enabled us to make significant improvements. The results of focusing on each metric can be seen by the improvement we were able to achieve in figures 4b–d.

Applying DevOps and Agile Principles at Scale

While starting with activity-based accounting and cycle-time drivers is probably the most accurate approach, it will quickly point you to the processes for maintaining always-releasable code and your planning processes, just as it did for us at HP.

Writing code is similar in large and small organizations, but the processes for planning it, integrating it with everyone else, qualifying it, and getting it to the customer are dramatically different. In almost every large, traditional organization, this is by far the biggest opportunity for improvement. Far too often these parts of the process take a lot of resources and time because traditional organizations tend

FIGURE 4D: STATE-OF-THE-ART FIRMWARE DEVELOPMENT MODEL

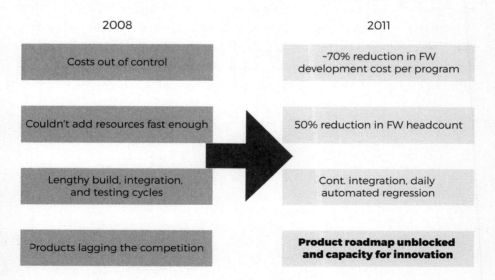

2008 — 2011

Costs out of control	~70% reduction in FW development cost per program
Couldn't add resources fast enough	50% reduction in FW headcount
Lengthy build, integration, and testing cycles	Cont. integration, daily automated regression
Products lagging the competition	**Product roadmap unblocked and capacity for innovation**

to plan details too far into the future and depend too much on manual testing and multiple code branches. The efforts required to keep these branches coordinated and tested tends to overwhelm most traditional organizations and keeps them from using frequent releases to get quick feedback from their customers. Additionally, if you are going to take advantage of the quick feedback from your customers, you will need to ensure your planning processes have been modified to provide a flexible response to what you learn.

Summary

It is difficult to address the unique and business-specific results that come out of activity-based accounting and cycle-time driver approach. Therefore, the rest of this book will focus on applying Agile and DevOps principles at scale to provide ideas and recommendations to address the traditional challenges of transforming these parts of your development process. Whether you do the detailed activity-based accounting and cycle-time view of your process or start with applying DevOps and Agile principles at scale, it is important that you begin with clear business objectives. This transformation is going to take a lot of effort, and if you don't have clear business objectives driving the journey, you can't expect the transformation to provide the expected business results. At HP we were able to get two to three times the improvement in business results because that was the focus of all our changes. If we couldn't see clearly how a change would help meet those goals, we did not waste any time with it, even though it might have been popular in the Agile community. It is this type of focus on the business objectives that enables the expected business results. These objectives also help in the organizational change management process, where you can constantly remind the team of where you are, where you are going, and the expected benefits.

⣿⣿⣿⣿ CHAPTER 4

ENTERPRISE-LEVEL CONTINUOUS IMPROVEMENT

After defining business objectives, the next important step in transforming your development process is creating an enterprise-level continuous improvement process. Executives need to work with their management chain and partners to lead this process because they are the only ones who can align the resources within the organization to drive the level of transformation that is required. They also have an end-to-end view of the value chain and are best positioned to bring all the resources of the organization to bear on a common plan for improving the development processes.

Executives can't just manage this transformation with metrics. Since software productivity is so hard to measure, they must continuously engage with the organization and its people throughout the journey to get a qualitative feel for what is and isn't working. This continuous improvement process is more than just making sure all the small Agile teams in the organization are doing retrospectives to become more effective. It requires creating a culture of continuous improvement where enterprise-level objectives are set and goals are defined for the iteration. Having iteration checkpoints with retrospectives and incorporating new ideas into the objectives for the next iteration are both essential parts of continuous improvement. Executives need to engage in the process to ensure you experience the most important principle of Agile development: learning and adjusting along the way.

Enterprise-Level Iteration Objectives

When you have a large organization delivering hundreds of stories per iteration, at the team level, the stories are important and meaningful to track. But for the executives, that level of detail is just too much noise, resulting in a strategy/plan that is an aggregate of details instead of a well-thought-out set of objectives. Exec-

FIGURE 5. MM30 CHECKPOINT STATUS

RANK	THEME	EXIT CRITERIA
0	Quality	- P1 open < 1wk - CAT 100% pass - L2 24hr response
1	1st bit release on new Arch for WinXP scanner	A) **Final P1 defects fixed** 2 remaining. B) Duration error rate per 10K: 0.3 (sim), 0.35 (emul), **0.4 (product)**
2	Ensuring common code stability on WinCE & the CE products supported	A) Customer accpt level (CAT) tests 100% passing on CE B) Test coverage appropriate for CE added to L1 (Terrese) C) All L2 pillars 98% pass – w/ coverage for high-value Product turn-on reqts for the CE products D) L4emu test pillars – LLFW (Arch), copy/PDL (Brian), PD (Hugh) E) Garnet L3 CAT in place with at least L4 CAT equivalence
3	Supporting the product reqs for the MIPS based products on CE	A) Calibration dependencies (Kimberly/Brian/Ted/Steve / Matt F) B) Print for an hour at speed to finisher with stapling (all) C) Copy for an hour **at speed** 35ppm (40ppm is at speed) D) **Enter/exit powersave (Steve / Mike)** Approved to push out to MM31 E) Mfg test suite exec on Coral **emulator with FIM support** (Terrese) F) **Automated FIM – no bash prompt (Steve)** Approved to push to MM31
4	Start porting CE code to ARM	A) Build single ARM system (Terrese) Feasibility proven. 2 DLL's to re-compile. B) High-level analysis of FW performance on ARM (Pat) Lowered priority.
5	Fleet Integr plan	Align on content for Coral/Garnet "slivers" of end-to-end agile test in ES. Overall plan in place. Need sliver details or will just deliver same as to PTO's.
BONUS		1st ARM/CE product - End-to-end boot, print, copy

■ Done   ■ **Not done**
■ Close enough

utives need to establish strategic objectives that make sense and that can be used to drive plans and track progress at the enterprise level. These should include key deliverables for the business and process changes for improving the effectiveness of the organization.

At HP we made sure we had a set of objectives that we used to drive the organization during each iteration. There were typically four to seven high-level objectives with measurable sub-bullets we felt were most important to achieve, things like shipping the next set of printers or taking the next step forward in our test automation framework. It also included things like improving our test passing rates, since stability had dropped, or a focus on feature throughput , since development was getting behind.

The table in figure 5 is a scrubbed version of the actual objectives from MM30, our 30th monthly iteration. During MM30 we were completing the rearchitecture of the codebase and getting ready to release the first scanner on Windows XPe with a MIPS processor. This required our highest priority to be completing the bit release and improving stability. We were also in the process of supporting product testing for the next generation of printers that were based on Windows CE and MIPS processors. This required our second highest priority to be improving the stability of the codebase on CE and getting the simulator automated testing in place. The third priority was addressing all the product-specific requirements of the new products in this release window. We also had the first prototypes of the next generation products showing up that were based on Windows CE and an ARM processor. This led to our fourth priority of ensuring we could port the common codebase to the ARM processor. Our fifth priority was getting the first XPe on MIPS processor products ready for system qualification on the final products.

While it includes some team-level stories, it more importantly focuses on the enterprise-level deliverables. Executives work with the organization to set these kinds of objectives so that everyone feels they are important and achievable. They also make sure the objectives are based on what the teams are actually doing and achieving. This kind of collaboration helps build a culture of trust.

These are very high-level strategic objectives that include business objectives and process improvements. Can you see how it is much more than just an aggregate of the team-level stories? Can you also see why everyone across the organization would have to make these their top priorities instead of team-level stories if we were really going to make progress?

These objectives provided an organization-wide set of priorities that drove work throughout the organization. If you were working on one of these top priorities, the organization understood people needed to help if you asked. Each team was expected to prioritize the team's stories that were required to meet these objectives. Once the team had met the strategic objectives, they were empowered to use the rest of their capacity to make the best use of their time and prioritize the team-level stories. This approach allowed for defining aligned objectives for the enterprise while also empowering the teams. It was a nice balance of top-down and bottom-up implementation.

Tracking Progress and Understanding Challenges

These objectives guided all our work. There was a website that aggregated all of our metrics and enabled tracking every objective down through the organization. The metrics would start at the overall organization, then cascade down to each section manager, and then down to each team. As executives, we would each start the morning at our desks spending 30–45 minutes reviewing these metrics, so we were able to know exactly how we were doing meeting these objectives and could identify where we were struggling. We did not have many status meetings or Scrum of Scrum meetings because the data was always at everyone's fingertips.

The leadership team would then spend most of their days walking the floor trying to understand where we were struggling and why. This is a new role for most executives and one we encourage executives to embrace if this process is going to be successful. We became investigative reporters trying to understand what was working and what needed to be improved. People wanted to meet the objectives we set and felt were reasonable at the beginning of the iteration, so something must have happened if they were struggling. These discussions around what got in the way were one of the most valuable parts of the process both in terms of learning what needed improving and in terms of changing the culture.

When high-level executives first started showing up at the desks of engineers that were struggling, it was intimidating for the engineers. After awhile, though, the engineers realized we were just there to help, and the culture started to change.

FIGURE 6: ENTERPRISE-LEVEL CONTINUOUS IMPROVEMENT

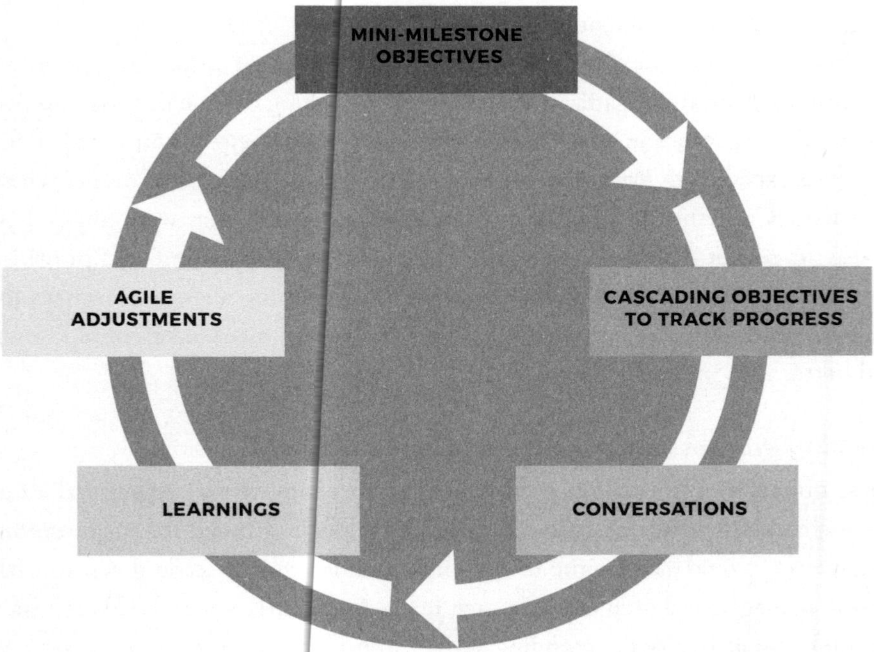

MINI-MILESTONE OBJECTIVES

AGILE ADJUSTMENTS

CASCADING OBJECTIVES TO TRACK PROGRESS

LEARNINGS

CONVERSATIONS

The engineers began sharing their ideas and making their struggles visible because they realized that the executives were there to provide help and were willing to make changes. **With this kind of trust comes transparency and with transparency comes a greater ability to fix issues quickly. As executives, we came to understand the importance of this culture shift.**

Adjusting Based on Feedback and Aligning for the Next Iteration

During the last week of our monthly iteration we would start evaluating what we could and could not get done in that iteration. We would also integrate what we learned about where the organization was struggling in setting the objectives for the next iteration. Objectives usually started out as a discussion between the program manager and the director with a notepad standing in front of a poster of the previous iteration objectives. In about 20 minutes, we would create a rough draft of objectives for the next iteration. We say "rough draft" because we had not yet gotten the perspectives and support of the broader organization. Over the next few days there were reviews in lab staff meetings, the section managers' meetings, and a project managers' meeting where we scrubbed and finalized the objectives into a list everyone felt was achievable and critical to our success. **We know that aligning the organization on enterprise iteration goals takes longer than most small Agile teams take to set objectives for an iteration, but for a large organization it felt like a good balance of driving strategy at the top and getting the buy-in and support from the troops.**

Summary

A culture of continuous improvement at the enterprise level is important for any large successful transformation. At HP, we never set off to implement a three-year detailed plan to transform our business. We just started with our business objectives and worked down a path of continuous improvement one month at a time. In the end, we looked back and realized we had delivered dramatic business results. It required setting enterprise-level objectives each iteration, tracking progress, and making the right adjustments for the next iteration. You are never going to know all the right answers in the beginning, so you are going to need an effective enterprise-level process for learning and adjusting along the way. An enterprise-level continuous improvement process is a key tool executives use for leading transformations and learning from the organization during the journey.

PLANNING & PRIORITIZED
BACKLOG

⊪⊪⊪CHAPTER 5
AGILE ENTERPRISE PLANNING

Convincing large, traditional organizations to embrace Agile principles for planning is difficult because most executives are unfamiliar with the unique characteristics of software development or the advantages of Agile. As we have discussed, they expect to successfully manage software development using a Waterfall planning and delivery process, just like they successfully manage other parts of their business. This approach, though, does not utilize the unique advantages of software or address its inherent difficulties. Software is infinitely flexible. It can be changed right up to the time the product is introduced. Sometimes it can be changed even later than that with things like software or firmware upgrades, websites, and software as a service (SaaS).

Software does have its disadvantages, too. Accurately scheduling long-term deliveries is difficult, and more than 50% of all software developed is either not used or does not meet its business intent. **If executives managing software do not take these differences into account in their planning processes, they are likely to make the classic mistake of creating detailed, inaccurate plans for developing unused features. At the same time they are eliminating flexibility, which is the biggest advantage of software, by locking in commitments to these long-range plans.**

Unique Characteristics of Software

Agile software development was created because traditional planning and project management techniques were not working. Unlike traditional projects, software is almost infinitely flexible. It's call SOFTware for a reason. At any time you can change it to do something different. At the other extreme, hardware is much more difficult and costly to modify. If you've ever lived through a full metal mask roll for a custom ASIC on a laser printer to resolve a design problem, you are fully aware of just how long, painful, and expensive this can be. A simple human error made during the ASIC design can result in a schedule slip of several months and cost overruns of $1M.

This same principle can be applied in most non-software projects. Once the two-by-fours are cut, they're not going to get any longer. Once the concrete is poured and dried, it's not going to change shape. The point is that if you're managing a construction project or a hardware design effort, you must do extensive requirements gathering and design work up front; otherwise, mistakes are very time-consuming and costly to fix. The project management discipline has evolved to match this lack of flexibility and minimize the likelihood of making these kinds of mistakes.

Software on the other hand, if managed and developed correctly, is less expensive and easier to change. The problem is that most software is managed using the same techniques that are applied to these other inflexible disciplines. In the software world we call it Waterfall development life cycle. By applying these front-end heavy management techniques to software development we limit ourselves in two ways.

First, we rob ourselves of software's greatest benefit: flexibility. Instead of doing extensive planning and design work that locks us into a rigidly defined feature set, we should take advantage of the fact that software can be quickly and easily modified to incorporate new functionality that we didn't even know about when we did the planning and scheduling several months prior. The software process, if done correctly, cannot only accept these late design changes, but can actually embrace and encourage them to ensure that the customers' most urgent needs are met, regardless of when they are discovered.

Second, we drive software costs up far higher than they should be. When software is developed using the Waterfall model, many organizations will spend 20–30% or more of their entire capacity to do the requirement gathering and scheduling steps. During these steps the software teams make many assumptions and estimates because every new software project you do is unique. It is unlike any other piece of software you already have. Even if you are rearchitecting or refactoring existing functionality, the implementation of the code is unique and unlike what you had before.

Compare this to remodeling your kitchen, where Waterfall planning works well. Your contractor has installed a thousand sinks, dishwashers, and cabinets. He will use the same nails, screws, and fittings that he has used before. His estimates of cost and schedule are based on years of experience doing the same activities over and over, finding similar issues. There is some discovery during the actual implementation, but it is much more limited. With software your teams have limited experience doing exactly what you're asking them to do. As a result, the actual implementation is filled with many discoveries and assumptions made up front that are later found to be incorrect when actual development begins.

Additionally, integration and qualification tends to uncover major issues late in the process. If the customer sees the first implementation of a feature months after development began and you then discover that you misunderstood what was wanted, or if the market has shifted and other features are now more important, you have just wasted a significant amount of time and money. It is far better to show the customer new functionality right as it becomes available, which is simply not possible using the Waterfall methodology.

Because software development is so different from how executives usually do business, it can take awhile to overcome resistance to applying Agile principles to the planning process. We can't stress enough that if you don't design your planning process correctly, it can end up using a lot of the capacity of the organization without providing much value.

Creating a planning process that embraces the Agile principles starts with executives understanding and accepting long-term predictability for software schedules. The curve depicted in figure 7 shows the accuracy of software planning for longer-range software deliveries of several months to several years. It graphs the accuracy of the plan versus the investment in planning. For a relatively small investment in planning, you can get a reasonable first pass at the plan. More investment can result in better accuracy up to a point, until you start reaching diminishing returns on your investment.

Most traditional organizations, when faced with the reality of just how inaccurate their software planning processes are, tend to react by investing more and more in planning. They do this because they are convinced that with enough effort they will make their plan accurate. It works for every other part of their business, so why not with software? The reality is that with software you are reaching a point of diminishing returns, and at that point the best way to learn more about the schedule is to start writing code. Once the code starts coming together, the team learns a lot more about their assumptions and can better define their schedule for shorter time frames. The other challenge with traditional organizations pushing for more accuracy in their

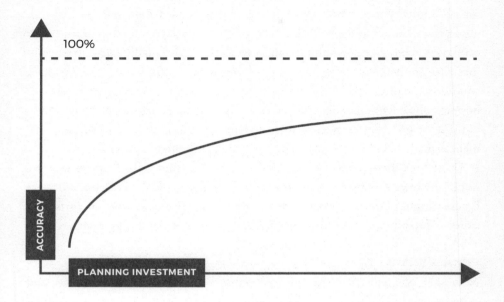

FIGURE 7: LONG-TERM PREDICTABILITY FOR SOFTWARE SCHEDULES

Do we really need the predictability of our current planning processes?
Are our current planning processes really that accurate?
50% of all software is never used or does not meet the business objectives!

100%

ACCURACY

PLANNING INVESTMENT

planning processes is that this push eats up valuable capacity the organization could be using for identifying and delivering actual business value. **Therefore, organizations need to decide whether their primary objective is to deliver long-term accurate plans to its executives or if it is to deliver business value to its customers.**

There are two other approaches traditional organizations tend to use when addressing this dilemma of long-term accuracy in plans. The first, used widely in most successful Waterfall organizations, is to put ample buffer into the schedule. This is typically defined as the time between a milestone like "functionality complete" and the software release. If the analysis shows the development is going to take six months, then commit to the delivery in nine to twelve months. The other is to commit to the schedule and when it is not on track, just add resources and work the Development teams night and day on a death march until the program ships.

In either case you are not changing the curve in the graph. Your schedule is still inaccurate. You are just trying to fight that reality with different techniques. Getting the management chain to acknowledge and accept the realities of this curve is the first step toward embracing the Agile planning principles and techniques.

Executives also need to understand that more than 50% of software developed is never used or does not meet its intended business objectives. That is the metric for the industry as a whole. Your company might be better, but even if your group is well above average, having 30% of all software you develop not meeting objectives is a big opportunity for improvement. Additionally, software capabilities that are defined for release 12–24 months in the future are likely to have conditions change, and even if properly delivered will not meet the then-current business objectives. Therefore, it makes more sense to capitalize on the flexibility of software and delay software feature decisions as late as possible so the commitment is made based on the most current understanding of the market.

Don't lock in your most flexible asset to commitments for features that are not likely to meet your business objectives. Embrace the flexibility of software by creating a planning process that is designed take advantage of software's unique flexibility so you can best respond to the ever-changing market.

Process Intent

Now that you have a better understanding of the unique characteristics of software, the key to designing a good software planning process in an enterprise is being very clear about the Process Intent. The planning process is used primarily to support different business decisions. So you should be clear about the decisions required and invest the least amount possible to obtain enough information to support these decisions.

While the curve of the graph shows it is hard to get a high level of accuracy for long-range plans, that does not mean that businesses can live without firm long-range commitments for software. The challenge is to determine what requires a long-term commitment and ensure these commitments don't take up the majority of your capacity. Ideally, if these long-term commitments require less than 50% of your development capacity, a small planning investment can provide the information required to make a commitment.

On the other hand, if these firm long-range commitments require 90–110% of the capacity, this creates two significant problems. First, when the inevitable discovery does occur during development, you don't have any built-in capacity to handle the adjustments. Second, you don't have any capacity left to respond to new discoveries or shifts in the market. In either case, if you do need to make a change, it is going to take an expensive, detailed replanning effort to determine what won't get done so you can respond to the changes.

The planning process also needs a view of the priorities across the teams. It should look across the organization so the most important things are being developed first. Otherwise, the individual teams are at risk of suboptimizing the system by developing capabilities the teams feel are important but are less important to the overall line of business they are supporting. There needs to be a process for moving people or whole teams across initiatives to ensure the right overall business priorities are being developed first.

The LaserJet Planning Example

An example from the HP LaserJet business can help clarify how this planning process can work. HP had to make significant investments in manufacturing capacity 12-plus months before the software or firmware development was complete, so being able to commit to shipping the product on time was critical. Before we completed the rearchitecting and reengineering of the development processes, porting the code to a new product and the testing required to release it was taking ~95% of the resources. This resulted in large investments in planning to ensure enough accuracy for committing to a product launch. To make matters worse, the organization wanted firm long-term commitments to every feature that Marketing considered a "MUST."

Additionally, Marketing had learned that if a feature was not considered a "MUST" then it was never going to happen, so almost everything became a "MUST" feature 12-plus months before the product was introduced, adding on another 50–55% of demand on capacity. This led to an organization that was trying to make long-term commitments with 150% of its capacity, requiring a large investment in planning to clarify what could and couldn't be done. When the planning was done and it was clear that not all the "MUST" features could be completed, we needed another planning cycle to prove the "MUST" features really couldn't be delivered—because after all, they were "MUST" features. This vicious cycle was taking precious capacity away from a team that could have been delivering new capabilities and products.

Breaking this logjam required a significant investment in the code architecture and development processes. When just porting the code to a new product and the release process was taking ~95% of the capacity, it was not realistic to create an effective long-range planning process. Therefore, we rearchitected the code so that porting to a new product did not require a major investment and we automated our testing so it was easier to release the code on new products. **These changes meant that the long-range commitments required from the business were taking less than 50% of our capacity. Additionally, we separated out the long-term manufacturing commitment requirements from the feature commitment decisions that could wait until later. Only then was it possible to develop a nice, lightweight, long-range planning process.**

This new planning process consisted of three approaches for different time horizons to support different business objectives and decisions. The goal was to avoid locking in capacity as long as possible but still support the decisions required to run the business. We worked to keep the long-range commitments to less than 50% of the capacity. For shorter time frames when there was less uncertainty, we would commit another 30%. Then for the last part of the capacity, we didn't really plan but instead focused on delivering to a prioritized backlog. This approach built in flexibility with reserved capacity to respond to the inevitable changes in the market and discoveries during development.

The first and longest range phase focused on the commitment to ship the product on a specific date. In this phase, the unique capabilities of the new printer were characterized and high-level estimations were put in place to ensure there wasn't anything that would preclude committing to an introduction date. Because this was taking less than 50% of the capacity, it did not require a lot of detailed rigor in the planning for introductions 12-plus months in the future.

The next phase focused on major marketing initiatives that the organization leaders wanted to target over the next six months. This involved the system engineers working with the Marketing leadership team to clarify at a high-level what capabilities they would like to message across the product line in the next marketing window. The system engineers would then roughly estimate the capacity left after commitments to shipping new products and the initiative's demands on the different teams in the organization. This leftover capacity is shown in the figure 8 as the number of engineering months available above each component team.

A relatively small group of system engineers created the analysis in figure 8 that shows an estimate of how many engineering months would be required from each component team for each initiative. You can see that initiatives 1–7 are almost certain to happen because all required teams easily have enough capacity to support the new features. Initiatives 12 and 13 weren't going to happen barring dramatic breakthroughs or increases in capacity, because based on this estimate component teams 3, 9, and 10 are out of capacity by initiative 10. Initiatives 8–11 are possible depending on the accuracy of the estimates and how development progresses. This approach also gives the management team a quick view of where

FIGURE 8

HIGH-LEVEL ESTIMATE—FW ENGINEERING MONTHS

RANK	INITIATIVE	Component 1 (25-30)	Component 2 (20-25)	Component 3 (30-40)	Component 4 (30-40)	Component 5 (20-30)	Component 6 (20-30)	Component 7 (20-30)	Component 8 (15-25)	Component 9 (20-30)	Component 10 (40-50)	Component 11 (20-30)	Other Items	TOTAL
1	Initiative A			21			5	3			1			30
2	Initiative B	3							4				17	24
3	Initiative C		5							1	2	1		9
4	Initiative D							10		2	2	2		16
5	Initiative E					20				3			5	28
6	Initiative F	23							5		6		2	36
7	Initiative G										2			2
8	Initiative H									5				5
9	Initiative I												3	3
10	Initiative J		20	27			17			21	39	17	9	150
11	Initiative K			3	30		3		3		14		12	65
12	Initiative L										2			2
13	Initiative M	3						10		6	6	6		31
		29	25	51	30	20	25	23	12	38	74	26	48	401

Time maxed-out

it makes the most sense to add capacity or move people across teams. An Agile planning process like this can give you the information you need for making the decisions required for that time horizon. Again, in this case you don't want to get locked into firm commitments for 100% of the capacity. So if the long-range plan committed to less than 50% of the capacity, this medium-range commitment should bring the total capacity used up to maybe 80%.

The next step in the planning process is used for shorter time ranges, from a couple of weeks to a few months. The goal is to understand in more detail exactly what is going to be delivered and when. In HP's case, there was not detailed planning other than a constant process of working through the prioritized backlog to break it down into requirements that were ~two weeks of engineering capacity. The team also did a very good job of making sure this ever-evolving backlog was carefully prioritized. Additionally, if business conditions changed or priorities needed to be adjusted, as long as the work had not started, it was okay to shift the priorities to the features most likely to deliver the expected business results.

Using the graph in figure 9, it was pretty easy to see what was and wasn't going to make different time horizons. You can see where the user story fits in the current backlog or queue on the right side of the graph and when it might be delivered based on the average throughput per release of 152 user requirements. If the feature is near the top 150 user requirements, it will most likely get delivered in the next release. If it is lower on the priority list it may take a couple of releases or might even get prioritized out of the backlog if the team comes up with new and better ideas. This process did not require a big planning investment and it ensured the team was delivering with 100% of the capacity to the most important features first while not locking in the team to firm commitments. This allowed the team to focus on delivery of business value with the flexibility in capacity to respond to uncertainty in schedule during delivery. It also enabled the Marketing group to respond to changing business conditions so that the features being defined and delivered in short planning horizons were less likely to be features that would never be used or would not deliver their intended business value.

The other change in the planning processes at HP was to minimize the requirements inventory. When we were not making long-term commitments to all the features, we did not have to invest in breaking down the requirements into details until we were much closer to starting development and knew the requirements were going to be used and much less likely to change. For

FIGURE 9: FUTURESMART FIRMWARE USER STORIES PER SPRINT
ESTIMATING SHORT-TERM FEATURES BASED ON DELIVERY

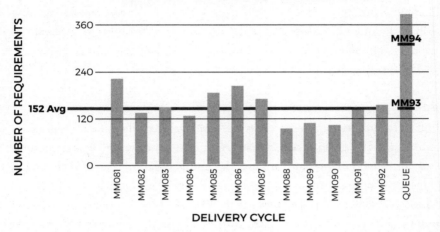

REQUIREMENTS THROUGHPUT BY ITERATION (MM)

the long-range commitments, the only requirements details created were the unique characteristics of the new printer. Then, in the initiative phase, the new features were only defined in enough detail to support the high-level estimates described in figure 9. Once these initiatives were getting closer to development, the system engineers would break the initiatives into more detailed user stories so that everyone better understood what was expected. Then right before development started, these user stories were reviewed in feature kickoff meetings with all the engineers involved in the development along with the Marketing person and system engineers. At this time the engineers had a chance to ask any clarifying questions or recommend potentially better approaches to the design. Then after everyone was aligned, the Development engineers would break down the high-level user stories into more detailed developer requirements, including their schedule estimates.

This just-in-time approach to managing our requirements provided a couple of key advantages. First, the investment in breaking the requirements down into more detail was delayed until we knew they would get prioritized for development. Second, since there were not large piles of requirements inventory in the system when the understanding of the market changed, there were not a lot of requirements that needed to be reworked.

The net result of all these changes is that planning went from taking ~20% of the organization's capacity down to less than 5%, freeing up an extra 15% of the capacity to focus on delivering business value. At the same time the management team had the information required to make business decisions for the different planning horizons. By delaying locking in all the capacity as long as possible, the organization was able use the inherent flexibility of software to increase the likelihood that the new features would be used and would deliver the intended business results.

Summary

Creating an enterprise planning process that leverages the principles of Agile starts with embracing the characteristics that are unique to software. It also requires planning for different time horizons and designing a planning process that takes advantage of the flexibility software provides. These changes in the planning processes can also help to eliminate waste in the requirements process by reducing the amount of inventory that isn't ever prioritized or requires rework as the understanding of the market changes. The HP LaserJet example shows how embracing the principles of Agile can provide significant business advantages. This example is not a prescription for how to do it, but it does highlight some important concepts every organization should consider.

First, the planning process should be broken down into different planning horizons to support the business decisions required for different time frames. Second, if the items that must have long-term commitments require more than 50% of your capacity, you should look for architectural and process improvements so that those commitments are not a major capacity driver. Third, since the biggest inherent advantage of software is its flexibility, you should not eliminate that benefit by allowing your planning process to lock in all of your capacity to long-range commitments—especially since these long-range features are the ones most likely to end up not meeting the business objectives. Lastly you should consider moving to just-in-time creation of requirements detail to minimize the risk of rework and investment in requirements that will never get prioritized for development.

The specifics of how the planning process is designed needs to be tuned to meet the needs of the business. It is the executives' role in the organization to appreciate how software development is different from the rest of their business and be willing to drive these new approaches across the organization. If they use the traditional approach of locking all their capacity to long-range commitments, then when there is discovery during development or in the market it will require expensive replanning cycles. Or even worse, the organization will resist changing their plans and deliver features that don't provide any value. Instead, executives need to get the organization to appreciate that this discovery will occur and delay locking in capacity as long as possible so they can avoid these expensive replanning cycles and take advantage of the flexibility software provides. Executives need to understand that the Agile enterprise planning process can provide significant competitive advantages for those companies willing to make the change and learn how to effectively manage software.

IIIIIII CHAPTER 6
BUSINESS OBJECTIVES SPECIFIC TO SCALING DEVOPS

APPLYING DEVOPS PRINCIPLES AT SCALE

Applying DevOps and Agile principles at scale in the enterprise requires developing processes that will enable the organization to economically release smaller batches of code on a more frequent basis. One of the biggest potential advantages of software products is that once a new feature is created, the marginal cost to manufacture and distribute it should ideally be next to nothing. If your development processes don't allow you to economically release small batches of new functionality, then you are not able to realize these full benefits of software. You also lose the benefits of receiving rapid feedback from your customers or market to see if the new capabilities are meeting expectations and understand outcomes to inform next steps.

This fundamental Agile principle of releasing frequently tends to get overlooked or ignored by organizations that approach Agile transformations by scaling teams. It has been so overlooked by these organizations that new practices called DevOps and Continuous Delivery (CD) have begun to emerge to address this gap. In DevOps, the objective is to blur the lines between Development and Operations so that new capabilities flow easier from Development into Production. On a small scale, blurring the lines between Development and Operations at the team level improves the flow. In large organizations, this tends to require more structured approaches like CD. Applying these concepts at scale is typically the source of the biggest breakthroughs in improving the efficiency and effectiveness of software development in large organizations, and it should be a key focus of any large-scale transformation and is a big part of this book.

In this book we purposefully blur the line between the technical solutions like CD and the cultural changes associated with DevOps under the concept of applying DevOps principles at scale, because you really can't do one without the other. DevOps and CD are concepts that are gaining a lot of momentum in the industry because they are addressing the aforementioned hole in the delivery process. That said, since these ideas are so new, not everyone agrees on their definitions.

CD tends to cover all the technical approaches for improving code releases and DevOps tends to be focused on the cultural changes. From our perspective you really can't make the technical changes without the cultural shifts. Therefore, for the proposes of this book we will define DevOps as processes and approaches for improving the efficiency of taking newly created code out of development and to your customers. This includes all the technical capabilities like CD and the cultural changes associated with Development and Operations groups working together better.

There are five main objectives that are helpful for executives to keep in mind when transforming this part of the development process so they can track progress and have a framework for prioritizing the work.

1. Improve the quality and speed of feedback for developers

Developers believe they have written good code that meets its objectives and feel they have done a good job until they get feedback telling them otherwise. If this feedback takes days or weeks to get to them, it is of limited value to the developers' learning. If you approach a developer weeks after they have written the code and ask them why they wrote it that way or tell them that it broke these other things, they are likely to say, "What code?," "When?," or "Are you sure it was me?" If instead the system was able to provide good feedback to the developer within a few hours or less, they will more likely think about their coding approach and will learn from the mistake.

The objective here is to change the feedback process so that rather than beating up the developer for making mistakes they don't even remember, there is a real-time process that helps them improve. Additionally, you want to move this feedback from simply validating the code to making sure it will work efficiently in production so you can get everyone focused on delivering value all the way to the customer. Therefore, as much as possible you want to ensure the feedback is coming from testing in an environment that is as much like production as possible. This helps to start the cultural transformation across Development and Operations by aligning them on a common objective.

The Operations team can ensure their concerns are addressed by starting to add their release criteria to these test environments. The Development teams then start to learn about and correct issues that would occur in production because they are getting this feedback on a daily basis when it is easy to fix. **Executives must ensure that both Development and Operations make the cultural shift of using the same tools and automation to build, test, and deploy if the transformation is going to be successful.**

2. Reduce the time and resources required to go from functionality complete or release branching to production

The next objective is reducing, as much as possible, the time and resources required to go from functionality complete or release branching to production. For large, traditional organizations, this can be a very lengthy and labor intensive process that doesn't add any value and makes it impossible to release code economically and on a more frequent basis. The work in this phase of the program is focused on finding and fixing defects to bring the code base up to release quality. Reducing this time requires automating your entire regression suite and implementing all-new testing so that it can be run every day during the development phase to provide rapid feedback to the developers. It also requires teaching your Development organization to add new code without breaking existing functionality, such that the main code branch is always much closer to release quality.

Once you have daily full-regression testing in place, the time from functionality complete or branch cut to production can go down dramatically because the historic effort of manually running the entire regression suite and finding the defects after development is complete has been eliminated. Ideally, for very mature organizations, this step enables you to keep trunk quality very close to production quality, such that you can use continuous deployment techniques to deploy into production with multiple check-ins a day.

This goal of a production-level trunk is pretty lofty for most traditional organizations, and lots of business customers would not accept overly frequent releases. Working towards this goal, though, enables you to support delivery of the highest-priority features on a regular cadence defined by the business instead of one defined by the development process capabilities. Additionally, if the developers are working on a development trunk that is very unstable and full of defects, the likely reaction to a test failure is "that's not my fault, I'm sure that defect was already there." On the other hand, if the trunk is stable and of high quality, they are much more likely to realize that a new test failure may in fact be the result of the code they just checked in. With this realization you will see the Development community begin to take ownership for the quality of the code they commit each day.

3. Improve the repeatability of the build, deploy, and test process

In most large, traditional organizations, the repeatability of the entire build, test, and deploy process can be a huge source of inefficiencies. For small organizations with independent applications, a few small scrum teams working together can easily accomplish this process improvement. For large organizations that have large groups of engineers working together on a leveraged code base or lots of different applications that need to work together, this is a very different story. Designing a deployment pipeline for how you build up and test these systems is important. It needs to be a structured, repeatable process, or you are going to end up wasting lots of time and resources chasing issues you can't find and/or trying to localize the offending code in a large, complex system. The objective here is to make sure you have a well-designed, repeatable process.

4. Develop an automated deployment process that will enable you to quickly and efficiently find any deployment or environment issues

Depending on the type of application, the deployment process may be as simple as FTPing a file to a printer or as complex as deploying and debugging code to hundreds or thousands of servers. If the application requires deploying to lots of servers, debugging the deployment process can be as complicated as finding code defects in a large system. Additionally, it can complicate the process of finding code issues because the system test failures can be either be code or deployment related. Therefore, it is important to create a deployment process that can quickly identify and isolate any deployment issues before starting system testing to find code issues.

5. Remove the duplication of work that comes from supporting multiple branches of similar code

Another important objective at this stage of the transformation is taking duplication out of the process. The goal is to have your marginal costs for manufacturing and deploying software to be almost zero. This starts to break down when you are working with more than one branch of similar code. Every time you find a code issue, you need to make sure it is correctly ported and working on every associated branch. It breaks down even more when your qualification requires any manual testing, which is expensive and time-consuming on these different branches.

There are lots of different reasons you will hear for needing different branches. Some reasons are customer driven. Other reasons for different branches include the belief that you need branches at different levels of stability or that you will have to bring in architectural changes and different branches make that easier. All these issues have been solved by organizations that have learned how to develop on one trunk and have realized the efficiencies of this approach. It will take time and will be an organizational change management challenge, but the duplicate work associated with multiple branches is a huge inefficiency in most large software development organizations. Every time you see a branch that lasts more than a couple of days, you should think of it as duplicate costs in the system impacting the inherent economical benefits of your software. Repeat this phrase until you become comfortable with it: "Branches are evil; branches are evil; branches are evil." If you are working in a branch-heavy organization, this may take some time to address, but every time you see a branch you should ask why it's there and look for process changes that will address the same need without creating branches.

Summary

Applying DevOps principles in the enterprise has huge advantages but can take several months to years, depending on the size of the organization. Therefore, you need a clear set of business objectives to help define priorities and track progress to ensure you implement the most valuable changes first.

Because it is not a physical device that has to be manufactured, software can deliver new capabilities with very low manufacturing and distribution costs. Most large, traditional organizations, though, have trouble taking advantage of software's flexibility because their development processes do not allow them to economically release small batches of new capabilities. Applying DevOps principles at scale is all about evolving the development process to make it easy to support frequent releases of new capabilities. In the next few chapters, we will show how to use these objectives to guide your implementation of applying DevOps principles at scale.

CREATING A CULTURE OF TRUNK DEVELOPMENT

While applying DevOps principles at scale requires good technical solutions, it is mostly about changing how people work. The technical solutions will require some finesse, but by far the biggest challenges will be around organizational change management and changing the culture. If executives can't get people to embrace the changes then it doesn't make sense to invest in the technical solutions. One of the most important cultural changes for aligning the work across the organization is having all the teams continually integrating and testing their code in a production-like environment.

Developing on Trunk

Getting a team to apply DevOps principles at scale is a challenge. In traditional organizations when you describe the vision and direction of large-scale CD on trunk to the engineers, they immediately will tell you why it won't work and how it will break when bringing in large changes. Most large, traditional organizations have been working so far away from CD for so long they can't imagine how it could possibly work. Therefore, the executive team is going to have to be very active in leading and driving this change. This happens by sharing the strategy/vision and showing how other traditional organizations have successfully transformed their development processes.

Executives need to understand that driving trunk to a stable state on a day-to-day basis in the enterprise is going to be a big change management challenge but this is probably the most important thing they can do to help coordinate the work across teams and improve the effectiveness of the organization. Once engineers have worked in an environment like this they can't imagine having worked any other way. Before they have experienced it, though, they can't imagine how it could ever work. Executives have to help lead this cultural transformation by starting with an achievable goal that includes a small set of automated tests, then increasing the minimal level of stability allowed in the system over time.

From a technical perspective the team will have to learn development practices like versioning services, rearchitecture through abstraction, feature flags, and evolutionary database design techniques.

In versioning services, you don't modify a service if it is going to break the existing code. Instead you create a new version of that service with the new capability. The application code is then written to ensure it calls the version of the service it is expecting. Then over time as all the application code is updated to the new service the old version of the service can then be deprecated. This approach enables always-releasable code and ensures the application layer and services layers of the code can move independently.

Rearchitecture through abstraction is a technique that allows you to refactor major parts of the code without breaking existing functionality. In this case, you find an interface in the code where you can start the refactoring. This interface should have a nice set of automated tests so you can ensure the new and old code will behave the same way with the rest of the system and you can test both the old and new code paths through this interface to make sure they are working. The old interface is used to keep the code base working until the new refactored code is ready. Then once the refactoring is complete, the old code is deprecated and the new code takes over running with the broader system.

Feature flags are another technique that enables developers to write new code directly on trunk but not expose it to the rest of the system by using feature flags to turn it off until it is ready.

Finally, evolutionary database is a technique like versioned services that enables you to make database schema changes without breaking existing functionality. Similar to versioning services, instead of modifying the existing data, you add new versions with the schema changes and then deprecate the old versions when all the applications are ready. These are not really technically challenging changes, but they are different ways of working that will require coordination and process changes across the development groups.

Leadership Team Responsibilities

If you are working to keep trunk stable with green builds in a large organization, making that "job 1" for everyone is not an easy task, and it is an important cultural shift that executives need to help facilitate. All it takes is a few developers not buying into the change to create a train wreck with long periods of broken builds and an inefficient process.

At HP we started with rules that were strongly enforced by the leadership team. The first was that if you were going to commit code, you were required to stick around until the build was complete with the automated acceptance tests passing (green). Failing to do so was considered a "lab felony." In four years this only happened twice, and in each case it led to the director having an expectation-setting conversation with the individual and their management chain. The second rule was making sure people were not continuing to commit code into a broken (red) build. This was considered a "lab misdemeanor" because it was potentially piling more bad code onto a broken build that people were working to get fixed. We had this problem because we started with a traditional continuous integration process that required everyone swarming a red build because this train wreck was blocking all the rest of the code from progressing down the deployment pipeline.

FIGURE 10: TRAIN WRECK BLOCKING CODE PROGRESSION

Setting these rules and driving the changes in behavior required a fair amount of focus and energy by the leadership team. We found that it was taking a lot of our change management capacity to keep the builds green. Therefore, over time we learned how to have our tools automatically enforce the behavior we wanted. We did this by creating gated commits or auto-revert.

Gated commits enabled us to constantly have green builds and avoid train wrecks of broken builds without using the management team's change management capacity. If a code commit or group of commits did not result in a green build, instead of having everyone swarm to fix the issue on the trunk, we gated

FIGURE 11: GATING COMMITS

the changes that caused the build to go red so they never made it onto trunk in the source code management (SCM) tool.

Instead of having a train wreck blocking code progressions on the tracks, the offending code was moved off the tracks, debugged, and fixed so the next builds could keep moving through the system. No one could commit on a red build because the commits ahead of you that caused the previous build to go red were simply pulled off to the side allowing those who made the commits to resolve the issues. The SCM contained the versions of code that resulted in the most recent green build and not the versions of code that resulted in a red build. The system picked up the next set of commits in the pipeline and kicked off the next build.

Instead of lab management walking around and asking engineers why they committed on a red build, we created a process that eliminated the problem. For those developers that had their code auto-reverted, the system would send them an e-mail saying their code was rejected because a certain set of tests had failed. They were then responsible for fixing the issue and recommitting the code. This gave the developers time to fix the issue correctly without the rest of the organization breathing down their necks while the defect blocked the entire deployment pipeline.

This process change and toolset had a few very big advantages. First, it kept the build from ever becoming blocked (red) so people could always commit code and have it flow to trunk. Second, it focused the impact of the failure to the smallest group of people possible. Now instead of the whole organization focusing on keeping the build green, the tools automatically enforced the change in behavior.

As you start working with your teams to begin implementing these DevOps principles at scale you can either start with your leadership using its change management capacity to drive the change or invest in process changes and the tooling to force the correct behavior. Both work, but we would recommend taking the time to setup auto-revert or gated commits to drive this change. It will take a little more time to get started, but the rollout will go so much more smoothly that it is worth it.

Shifting Mindsets

When we set out the vision of one main branch for all current and future products using continuous integration at HP, most of the engineers thought we had lost our minds. They would avoid making eye contact when we walked down the hall and were just hoping at some point we would snap back to reality. It was especially challenging for our technical lead of the build, test, and release process. He really wanted to engage us in the branching discussion. Every time he did we would say "we aren't going to branch." It got to the point where he probably wore out a thesaurus trying to find ways to talk about branching without using the *B*-word.

Once we had the deployment pipeline up and really working, people got used to working that way and appreciated its advantages. Engineers would see bringing in big changes on trunk as the best way of getting real-time feedback on how their code would work with the rest of the system. As the rearchitecture came to completion and we were close to releasing our first product, we approached the lead about being ready to branch. His response was that we shouldn't branch and lose all the efficiencies of having an organization-level deployment pipeline giving real-time feedback to the developers on one trunk. The next time we saw him he had come back from a river trip down the middle fork of the Salmon with a "Flying B Ranch" hat from the local airstrip and ranch. He walked up with the hat and said, "We don't need no stinking B-Ranch."

We like this lesson for two reasons: First and foremost it is our personal belief that this is the biggest opportunity for improving development productivity in the enterprise. Second, it shows the big shift in mindset that needs to occur. The lead went from the biggest nonbeliever to the biggest supporter of the approach. Until engineers have worked in this type of environment, they will never believe it can work. Once they have developed in this type of environment, however, they can't imagine ever going back. Over the years we have had several different engineers that, after leaving HP, called to talk about how backward development is in their new companies. They complain they are not nearly as effective because the feedback is non-existent and it is very hard to release code into production.

Summary

Transforming software development processes in a large organization is a big change management challenge. While technology can help, if the executives are not willing to lead and drive cultural changes like developing on trunk, then no amount of technology is going provide the necessary breakthroughs. Developers need to know they can develop stable code on trunk and should take responsibility for ensuring the code base is always close to release quality by keeping the builds green. They also need to understand the objective of the organization is to optimize the delivery of new capabilities all the way out to the customer not just on their desktops. Ensuring each developer is responsible for making sure every check-in works in this production-like environment will start the cultural shift of aligning Development and Operations on a common objective.

Keeping builds green can be done solely by process change and leadership enforcement. Ideally, though, you should design your continuous integration process to help drive the required changes in behavior. This is probably one of the biggest things you can do to improve the productivity of software development in large organizations. Most engineers, however, will argue initially it can't be done. Only by working in this type of environment will they understand how much more productive it is. Then they can't imagine working any other way. The challenge for executives is leading people on the journey from nonbelievers to champions of the new way of working. It is important for executives to understand early on if the organization is embracing this cultural change, because if it doesn't, all the investments in technical changes will be a waste of time.

‖‖‖‖‖CHAPTER 8
ENSURING A SOLID FOUNDATION

Before applying DevOps principles at scale it is important for executives to ensure they are working from a solid foundation and that they understand the fundamentals currently in place in their organization, or else they will needlessly struggle to transform their development processes.

The first fundamental is clean architectures that enable smaller teams to work independently in an enterprise and make it possible to find defects with fast running unit or subsystem tests. The second is build and the ability to manage different artifacts as independent components. The third is test automation.

Applying DevOps and Agile principles at scale requires lots of automated testing. Expect to create, architect, and maintain at least as much test code and automation scripts as you create production code. Soundly architected test code leads to soundly architected production code that is easy to understand and maintain. If done well, this is a key enabler. If done wrong, it can turn into a maintenance nightmare that will cause a lot of problems, and the tests will not quickly localize coding issues.

Architecture

Executives need to understand the characteristic of their current architecture before starting to apply DevOps principles at scale. Having software based off of a clean, well-defined architecture provides a lot of advantages. Almost all of the organizations presenting leading-edge delivery capabilities at conferences have architectures that enable them to quickly develop, test, and deploy components of large systems independently. These smaller components with clean interfaces enable them to run automated unit or subsystem tests against any changes and to independently deploy changes for different components. In situations like this, applying DevOps principles simply involves enabling better collaboration at the team level.

On the other hand, large, traditional organizations frequently have tightly coupled legacy applications that can't be developed and deployed independently.

Ideally traditional organizations would clean up the architecture first, so that they could have the same benefits of working with smaller, faster-moving independent teams. The reality is that most organizations can't hold off process improvements waiting for these architectural changes. Therefore, executives are going to have to find a pragmatic balance between improving the development processes in a large, complex system and fixing the architecture so the systems are less complex over time. We encourage you to clean up the architecture when and where you can, and we also appreciate that this is not very realistic in the short term for most traditional organizations. As a result, we will focus on how to apply DevOps principles at scale assuming you still have a tightly coupled legacy architectures. In these situations where you are coordinating the work across hundreds to thousands of people, the collaboration across Development and Operations requires much more structured approaches like Continuous Delivery.

Embedded software and firmware has the unique architectural challenge of leveraging common stable code across the range of products it needs to support. If the product differences are allowed to propagate throughout the code base, the Development team will be overwhelmed porting the code from one product to another. In these cases it is going to be important to either minimize the product-to-product hardware differences and/or isolate the code differences to smaller components that support the product variation. The architectural challenge is to isolate the product variation so as much of the code as possible can be leveraged unchanged across the product line.

The Build Process

The next step in creating a solid foundation is to validate that the build process will enable you to manage different parts of your architecture independently. Some organizations do not have this fundamental in place. There is a simple test that can evaluate how ready you are with your build process.

Start by creating an architectural drawing that describes how you think about your artifacts, something similar to figure 12. Now create a fully integrated system using these components and ensure this build is "green" by running a few basic automated tests. Next, determine if you can recover from a bad component of your architecture making it into the next build. If version 2 of all the components come together in this second build, but component *B* causes the build to go red, you need to be able to revert back to version 1

FIGURE 12: ENSURING THE ARCHITECTURE/BUILD SYSTEM IS READY

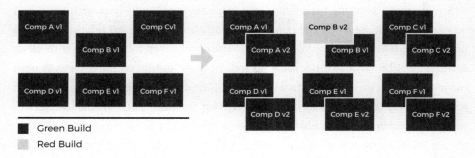

of component *B* and keep version 2 of everything else to get back to a green build. If you can do this with all the different components then you have this basic fundamental covered. If not, then you have some work to do in terms of breaking build dependencies between the different components before moving forward and applying DevOps principles.

This idea may seem simple, but it is a very basic building block because keeping the system stable requires building up and testing large software systems in a structured manner with different stages of testing and artifact promotion. If we are thinking of these artifacts as independent entities but in reality can't manage them that way, then we are not set up for success. If your software does not pass this simple test you need to start with fixing your build process and modifying your architecture to ensure that all components can be built and deployed into testing environments independent of the others.

Test Automation

A large amount of test automation is necessary when changing the development processes for large, traditional organizations. Without a solid foundation here, your feedback loops are going to be broken and there won't be an effective method for determining when to promote code forward in your pipeline. Writing good test automation is even more difficult than writing good code because it requires strong coding skills plus a devious mind to think about how to break the code. It is frequently done poorly because organizations don't give it the time and attention that it requires. Because we know it is important we always try to focus a lot of attention on test automation. Still, in almost every instance we look back on, we wish we had invested more because it is so critical.

You just can't keep large software systems stable without a very large number of automated tests running on a daily basis. This testing should start with unit- and services-level testing which are fairly straightforward. Ideally, you would be able to use these tests to find all of your defects. This works well for software with clean architectures but tends to not work as well in more tightly coupled systems with business logic in the user interface (UI) where you need to depend more on system level-based UI testing. In this case, dealing with thousands of automated tests can turn into a maintenance nightmare if they are not architected correctly. Additionally, if the tests are not designed correctly, then you can end up spending lots of time triaging failures to localize the offending code. Therefore, it is very important that you start with a test automation approach that will make it efficient to deal with thousands of tests on a daily basis. A good plan includes the right people, the right architecture, and executives who can maintain the right focus.

Test Environment

Running a large number of automated tests on an ongoing basis is going to require creating environments where it is economically feasible to run all these tests. These test environments also need to be as much like production as possible so you are quickly finding any issues that would impact delivery to the customer. For websites, software as a service, or packaged software this is fairly straightforward with racks of servers. For embedded software or firmware this is a different story. There the biggest challenge is running a large number of automated tests cost-effectively in an environment that is as close as possible to the real operational environment.

Since the code is being developed in unison with the product it is typically cost prohibitive, if not impossible, to create a large production-like test farm. Therefore, the challenge is to create simulators and emulators that can be used for real time feedback and a deployment pipeline that builds up to testing on the product. A simulator is code that can be run on a blade server or virtual machine that can mimic how the product interacts with the code being developed.

The advantage here is that you can set up a server farm that can quickly run thousands of hours of testing a day in a cost-effective way. The disadvantage is that it is not fully representative of your product, so you are likely to continue finding different defects as you move to the next stages of your testing. The objective here is to speed up and increase the test coverage and provide feedback to enable developers to find and fix as many defects as possible as early and thus as cheaply as possible. The simulator testing is fairly effective for finding defects in the more software-like parts of your embedded solution.

The challenge is that lots of products include embedded firmware running on custom ASICs. In this case, it is almost impossible to find defects in the interactions between the hardware and firmware unless you are running the code on the custom ASICs. This is the role of emulators. It is like the simulator in that it is code that mimics the product, but in this case it includes the electronics boards from the product with the custom ASICs but does not include the entire product. This is incrementally better than simulator testing because it is more like production. The challenge here is that these are more expensive to build and maintain than the simulator-based generic blade servers. Additionally, early in the development cycle the new custom ASICs are very expensive and in limited supply. Therefore, the test environments for the deployment pipeline are going to require a balance of simulators and emulators.

Finally, since these emulator environments are still not fully production-like, there will still need to be testing on the product. Creating processes for enabling small-batch releases and quick feedback for developers is going to require large amounts of automated testing running on the code every day. The challenge for embedded software and firmware is that this is not really practical on the product. **Therefore, robust simulator and emulators that can be trusted to quickly find the majority of the defects are a must. Executives will need to prioritize and drive this investment in emulators and simulators because too often embedded organizations try to transform development processes with unreliable testing environments, which will not work.**

Designing Automated Tests for Maintainability

A big problem with most organizations is that they delegate test automation task to the quality assurance (QA) organization and ask their manual testers to learn to automate what they have been doing manually for years. Some organizations buy tools to automatically record what the manual testers are doing and just play it back as the automated testing, which is even worse.

The problem with record and playback is that as soon as something on the UI or display changes, tests begin to fail and you have to determine if it is a code defect or a test defect. All you really know is that something changed. Since new behavior frequently causes the change, organizations get in the habit of looking to update the test instead of assuming it found a defect. This is the worst-case scenario for automated testing: where developers start ignoring the results of the tests because they assume it is a test issue instead of a code issue.

The other approach of having manual testers writing automated tests is a little better, but it has a tendency to result in brittle tests that deliver very long scripts that just replicate the manual testing process. This works fine for a reasonable number of tests when the software is not changing much. The problem, as we will demonstrate in the example below, comes when the software starts to change and you have thousands of tests. Then the upkeep of these tests turns into a mainte-nance nightmare. Whenever the code changes, it requires going through all the thousands of tests that reference that part of the software to make sure they get the right updates. In this case, organizations start to ignore the test results because lots of tests are already failing due to the QA team not being able to keep all their tests running and up to date.

The best approach for automated testing is to pair a really good development architect that knows the fundamentals of object-oriented programing with a QA engineer that knows how code is manually tested in the current environment. They can then work together to write a framework for automated testing.

A good example can be found in the book *Cucumber & Cheese: A Tester's Workshop* by Jeff Morgan. He shows how to create an object-oriented approach to a test framework using a puppy adoption website as an example. Instead of writing long monolithic tests for different test cases that navigate the website in similar ways, he takes an object-oriented approach. Each page on the website is represented by a page object model. Each time the test lands on that page there is a data magic gem that automatically randomly fills in any data required for that page. The test then simply defines how to navigate through the website and what to validate. With this approach, when a page on the website changes, that one-page object model is the only thing that needs to change to update all the tests that reference that page. This results in tests that are much less brittle and easier to maintain.

Using Page Object Models and other similar techniques will go a long way towards reducing your test development and maintenance costs. However, if your approach is to move fully to automated testing, the use of Page Object Models will be insufficient to drive your maintenance costs to an acceptable level. There are some additional techniques and processes that you will need to put in place.

Creating a Test Results Database

As discussed above, the first step in automated testing is to make sure the framework is stable and maintainable. The next step is ensuring there is a good tool for managing and reporting the test results. When there are tens to hundreds of automated tests running every day it is pretty easy to debug and triage all the failing tests. When the number of tests gets larger this approach is not very practical or effective. Managing this number of tests requires using a statistical approach to driving up test passing rates and stability. It also requires grouping the tests that are associated with different parts of the code base and designing the tests so they quickly localize the code issues. These test results then need to be in a tool or database that allows you to look at pass rates across different builds and test stages.

Designing Automated Tests to Quickly Localize Defects

We mentioned that one of the most common mistakes that organizations make when moving from manual to automated testing is to take their existing QA teams and simply have them start automating their existing manual scripts. This approach will cause some serious issues and will prevent you from having a cost-effective testing process. Since we've fallen into this pit a few times ourselves, we want to make sure that you are aware of the issues with this approach so that you can avoid them.

An example that will help illustrate the issues with automating manual test scripts is a large e-commerce website with new, added functionality that allows them to accept a new brand of credit card for payment. We want some tests that demonstrate that you can actually checkout and purchase a product using this new type of card.

To test this, our manual tester will go to the homepage of our website. From there they might search for a product using keyword search, and after finding and selecting a product, they will add it to the cart. From there they might go to the cart and see if the product they selected is the one that actually ended up in the cart. Next, they might sign in as a registered user so that they can determine if the loyalty points functionality will work using this new brand of credit card. To sign in as a registered user, they will have to enter their username and password. Now they are signed in and can add this new brand of credit card to their account and see if the website now accepts it as a valid form of payment. Assuming so, they're now ready to checkout. They click on the checkout button and land on the checkout page. Since they're logged in as a registered user, their name, address, and phone number should be prepopulated in the correct fields on the page. After validating this information the manual tester is now ready to do the part of the test that we have been waiting for: Can I select this new brand of credit card as my form of payment and actually purchase the product I selected?

The problem with automating this script is that the new automated test can fail for any number of reasons that have nothing to do with the new credit card or the checkout functionality. For example, if keyword search is not working today, this checkout test will fail because it can't find a product to put in the cart. If the sign in functionality is broken, the test will fail because it can't get past this stage of the test. Because this new test was written to validate our new functionality and it failed, the responsibility to triage this test failure lands upon the team developing the new credit card capability.

In reality, there will be many of these tests, some with valid and invalid credit card numbers, some that attempt to purchase a gift card, and some that attempt to purchase a product, but ship it to an alternate address. The list goes on. The result will be that on any given day our team could walk in to discover that most of their test suite that was working yesterday is now failing. As they begin to triage each failing test, they quickly learn that most are not failing because of the new functionality that was supposed to be tested, but because something else in the system is broken. Therefore, they can't trust the test failure to quickly localize the cause of the failure. It was designed and labeled as a test to checkout with a new credit card, and it is not until someone manually debugs the failure that it can be determined it is due to a code failure somewhere else in the system. Tests that are designed this way require a lot of manual intervention to localize the offending code. Once you start having thousands of tests you will realize this is just not feasible. The tests need to be written so that they are easy to update when the code changes, but they also need to be written so that they quickly localize the offending code to the right team.

One of the best and most important tools at your disposal to enable efficient triage is component-based testing. Think back to the architectural drawing that was referenced earlier in this chapter. What you want is a set of automated tests that fully exercise each component without relying on the functionality of the other components. In the traditional Waterfall method, we called this subsystem testing, and we expected each component or subsystem team to mock out the system around them and then test their component. Once all components were tested in this way, we moved on to the integration phase and put them all together and began system testing.

However, it is now possible to develop an automated testing framework that allows you to isolate the various components of the system, even when the system is fully integrated and deployed. Using our new credit card for a checkout example again, what we really want to do is start the test on the URL associated with the checkout page and to already have the user signed in and products loaded into the cart. We don't want to exercise the website to get all this data in place. We want the automation framework to do this work for us. With manual testing there is no way for this to happen. The tester has no choice but to walk through the entire workflow, end to end. However, a test automation framework can be built out that will do all of these things for you and allow your automated tests to exercise just the functionality you want to test. If our checkout tests and automation framework support the ability to test just the checkout functionality, things begin to change in a couple of very positive ways.

First, if these componentized tests begin to fail, you have a high level of assurance that the functionality that is broken is actually the functionality that the test is designed to exercise. When the team begins to triage the test failures, the likelihood that it is not their failure has decreased dramatically. The team will now quickly learn to pay attention to the test results because a pass or fail is much more likely to be an accurate representation of the state of their functionality.

The second big change is in your ability to statistically analyze your test metrics. When your automated test suite consists of a large number of tests that are just an automated version of your manual tests, it is very difficult to look at a large number of test results each day and determine which functionality is working and which functionality is broken. Even if you organize these tests into components, you will not be able to determine the status of each component. Remember from our example: when your checkout tests are all failing, you don't know if the problem is in the checkout functionality or not. You have no idea what is broken.

If instead you take a component-based approach of designing and grouping tests, then you can quickly localize a drop in pass rates to the offending code without a lot of manual triage intervention. This makes it feasible to efficiently respond to the thousands of automated tests that will be running every day.

Using Test Automation as Documentation

There is one more fundamental issue that involves automated testing as well as the actual code development process and is associated with the requirement- gathering and documentation process. In most large organizations, requirements are gathered from Marketing or some other part of the business. The software teams don't just dream up some new features and go implement them. The problem is that these requirements get gathered and distributed to the Development team, who go about their work of developing code and testing for this new functionality. Invariably, the various teams interpret these requirements differently. The Development teams put functionality in place that doesn't match what the test does, and when the teams go back to the business for clarification, they often discover that neither the developers nor the testers got it right. This leads to the Waterfall practice of more and more requirement reviews and estimating how long it will take to get something done.

The problem is amplified in many organization that are affected by things like the Sarbanes-Oxley Act, which necessitates requirements be associated with a piece of code and the tests that were used to validate that the code matches the requirement and are correct. Any software that deals with financial transactions or that drives things like medical devices comes under close scrutiny. Associating written requirements (specifications) to actual software and tests can be a time-consuming, expensive, and difficult process.

However, there are now tools and processes in place to significantly reduce the impact in this area. Most of the tools focus on creating specifications in an executable form. The idea is to have the business write the specification in an executable form so the automated test and the specification are the same thing. On the test side of the house, Cucumber is an excellent example. The Cucumber framework uses a Feature File, which is in an easy English readable format. The Feature File is the specification and is designed in such a way that it can be easily created by non-programmers. The Feature File is also executable code that is consumed by the test automation framework. Instead of writing language-based specifications, the specifications can now be written in such a way that they actually become the automated tests. This eliminates the need to manually associate specifications and code. It tests to meet audit requirements and gets everyone working off a common definition of the automated test from the very beginning.

Summary

Transforming the software development practices of large, traditional organizations is a very big task, which has the potential for dramatic improvements in productivity and efficiency. This transformation requires a lot of changes to how the software is developed and deployed. Before going too far down this path, it is important to make sure there is a solid foundation in place to support the changes. Executives need to understand the basic challenges of their current architecture and work to improve it over time. The build process needs to support managing different artifacts in the system as independent entities. Additionally, a solid, maintainable test automation framework needs to be in place so developers can trust the ability to quickly localize defects in their code when it fails. Until these fundamentals are in place, you will have limited success effectively transforming your processes.

CONTINUOUS DELIVERY

Applying DevOps principles at scale for a business that requires deploying code across multiple servers has unique challenges that are best addressed through Continuous Delivery. Jez Humble and David Farley developed this approach and documented it in detail in their book *Continuous Delivery: Reliable Software Releases through Build, Test, and Deployment Automation.* The details for your engineers are best found there. We will provide a brief summary for executives here because CD is so important to transforming development processes for these businesses. It will also include things we learned while transforming a large organization and discussions with Humble during our journey that were not in their book.

Continuous Delivery Definitions

Continuous Delivery is a fundamentally different approach to development and operations that automates as much of the configuration, deployment, and testing processes as possible and puts it all under a revision control. This is done to ensure the repeatability of the process across multiple servers and deployment environments. The automation helps to eliminate human errors, improves consistency, and supports increased frequency of deployments. As pointed out in *Continuous Delivery*, initially these processes are very painful. Nonetheless, you should increase their frequency to force you to fix all the issues.

When the frequency of the build and deployment process is fairly low, your organization is able to use brute force to work through these issues. When you increase the frequency, this is no longer possible. These issues that have been plaguing your organization for years will become much more visible and painful, requiring permanent automated solutions. Putting this automation under revision control enables tracking changes and ensuring consistency. The core pieces of Continuous Delivery you need to know are: continuous integration, scripted environments, scripted deployments, evolutionary database design, test automation, deployment pipeline, and orchestrator.

Continuous integration is a process that monitors the source code management tool for any changes and then automatically triggers a build and the associated automated build acceptance testing. This is required to ensure the code maintains a certain base level of stability and all changes are being integrated often to find conflicts early.

Scripted environments is an approach that creates a script that can be run against a server or virtual machine to configure all the settings from the operating system to the container. This is very different from what happens in most traditional organizations, where people are able to log onto servers and make changes required to get the application working. When people manually make changes, it is easy to get different servers across production or the deployment pipeline in different states of configuration. This results in seeing different issues as the code is moved through the deployment pipeline and having flaky issues based on different servers with the same application having different configurations. In this situation, a system test can become intermittent and begin to flicker. Even with exactly the same application code, a test will pass in one environment but fail in another because it is misconfigured in some subtle way. This tends to make the triage process very difficult, because it is hard to reproduce the problem when it only occurs on one of several servers hosting a common component. Scripted environments fixes this by having every server configured off of a common script that is under revision control. This ensures every server across the system has the exact same configuration.

Scripted deployment is a process for automating the deployment across all of the environments. This process deploys and configures the applications. Ideally, it also tests the deployments to ensure they were successful. This automation is also put under revision control so that it is repeatable day-to-day and server-to-server.

Evolutionary database design (EDD) is an approach for managing database changes to ensure that schema changes won't ever break your application. It also includes tools that put the database changes under revision control and can automatically update the database in any environment to the desired version of the configuration. The details are provided in a great book by Scott W. Ambler and Pramod J. Sadalage called *Refactoring Databases: Evolutionary Database Design*. It shows how to keep your application in an always-releasable state by never altering rows or columns but rather adding new versions of the rows or columns with the new schema changes. The application then ensures it is calling the version of the schema it was expecting when the code was written. Once the code in the application is updated to call the new version of the database schema, the old rows or columns are deleted. This approach allows you to keep your application in an always-releasable state and enables you to decouple application code changes from your database schema changes.

Deployment pipeline defines how new code is integrated into the system, deployed into different environments, and promoted through various stages of testing. This can start with static code analysis and unit testing at the component level. If these tests pass, the code can progress to a more integrated application-level testing with a basic build acceptance-level testing. Once these build acceptance tests are passing, the code can progress to the next stage, typically full regression and various forms of non-functional testing like performance and security testing. If full regression and non-functional testing results reach an acceptable pass rate, the code is ready to deploy into production. The deployment pipeline in CD defines the stages and progression model for your software changes.

Orchestrator is a tool that coordinates all of this automation. It enables you to call scripts to create new environments on a set of virtual machines with scripted environments, deploy code to that environment using scripted deployment, update the database schema with EDD, and then kick off automated testing. At the end of the automated testing, if everything passes, it can move this version of the applications and scripts forward to the next stage of the deployment pipeline.

Continuous Delivery Architecture

These definitions show the different pieces that need to come together to create a Continuous Delivery pipeline. These different pieces can be in different tools or, at times, in the same tool. That said, it makes sense to think of all the core pieces of CD as different and distinct activities so you can ensure that you are architecting CD correctly. Additionally, you want to make sure you are using an object-oriented approach to creating these scripts so that you don't end up with big, long, monolithic scripts that are brittle and hard to maintain. A CD pipeline can be created to work with monolithic scripts, and this might even be the best approach for small initiatives. That said, as you work to scale these processes across large organizations, it is important to take a more object-oriented approach. Think of the orchestrator as a different component that abstracts away the business logic of the deployment pipeline. It defines what scripts to call and when to call them to avoid creating too much complexity in the basic scripts. It also helps to think of grouping the scripts into common objects that can be leveraged if called by the orchestrator in the right order to support several different stages and roles in the deployment pipeline. Proper use of the orchestrator should enable the other components to have common scripts that can be leveraged for a variety of things.

**FIGURE 13: CONTINUOUS DELIVERY
PICKING THE RIGHT TOOL FOR THE JOB**

Orchestrator				
Trigger	Scripted Environment	Deployment	EDD	Auto Testing

Once you have thought through what tools to use for each process, it is important to think through how to architect scripted environments and scripted deployments. **The objective is to leverage, as much as is possible, a well-architected set of common scripts across different stages in the deployment pipeline from Development to Production.** These scripts need to be treated just like application code that is being developed and promoted through the deployment pipeline. Ideally you would want the exact same script used in each stage of the deployment pipeline.

While ideal, using the same script is frequently not possible because the environments tend to change as you progress up the deployment pipeline on the way to the full production environment. Therefore, your architectural approach needs to address how to handle the differences across environments while creating one common script that can be qualified and promoted through the deployment pipeline. This typically is accomplished by having one common script where variables are passed in to define the differences between the environments.

If this approach is not used, you are at risk of having large monolithic scripts that are different for each environment. When this occurs, even if these are being managed within an SCM, they tend to have very similar code being held in different branches that are difficult to keep consistent and tend to break. This ignores the basic principle of having a common script that is defined and qualified in the early stages of the deployment pipeline, then progressed forward to production and lacks the consistency that scripted environments is intended to address. Therefore, it is important to make sure your scripts for environments are architected correctly. Once they are, you have a process for defining an environment and having it replicated consistently across the deployment pipeline.

Executives need to ensure these technical changes happen because they start the cultural change of getting Development and Operations working with the same tools on common objectives. If the technical approaches are allowed to deviate, then you won't get the cultural alignment that is required for a successful transformation.

FIGURE 14: SCRIPTED ENVIRONMENT ARCHITECTURE

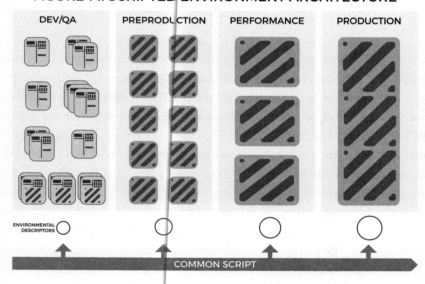

These same architectural concepts should apply for scripted deployments. Depending on the tool you chose, the process for defining environment differences for a common deployment script may be already built-in. If not, it is important to think through how to apply this architectural principle so you don't end up with long, monolithic scripts that are hard to maintain and not consistent across the deployment pipeline.

Post-Deployment Validation

The other key principle to include as part of the scripted deployment process is creating post-deployment validation tests to ensure the deployment was successful on a server-by-server basis. The traditional approach is to create environments, deploy the code, and then run system tests to ensure it is working correctly. The problem with this approach is that once a system test fails, it leads to a long and painful triage process. The triage process needs to determine if the test is failing due to bad code, a failed deployment, or other environmental differences. The scripted environment process ensures environmental consistency. This still leaves differentiating between code and deployment issues, which can be challenging. The scripted deployment process ensures the same automated approach is used for every server; however, it does not naturally ensure the deployments were successful for every server or that the various servers can actually interface with one another as expected. This becomes especially problematic when the deployment only fails for one of several common servers, because this leads to the system tests failing intermittently, depending on if that run of the tests happens to hit the server where the deployment failed. When this happens, it results in a very long and frustrating triage process to find the bad server and/or routing configurations amongst tens to hundreds of servers.

The good news is that there is a better approach. There are techniques to isolate code issues from deployment issues during the deployment process. You can create post-deployment validations to ensure the deployment was successful and localize the offending deployment issues down to the fewest number of potentially offending servers or routing devices as quickly as possible. Each step in the process is validated before moving on to the next step. Once the servers and routers are configured, there should be tests to ensure that the configuration has occurred correctly. If not, fix the issues before deploying the code.

The next step is to validate that the deployment was successful for every server individually. This can be done by automatically checking log files for warnings or errors and writing specific tests to ensure the deployment was successful. These checks should be done for every server and routing configuration before starting

FIGURE 15A: FINDING THE OFFENDING COMPONENT QUICKLY IMPROVES PRODUCTIVITY

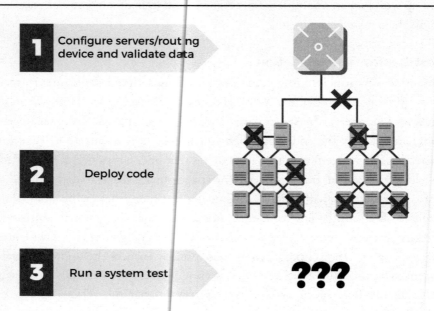

1 Configure servers/routing device and validate data

2 Deploy code

3 Run a system test

???

any system testing. Once each of these steps is complete, the system tests can start. The idea here is to define and automate the deployment pipeline such that it is isolating issues so that you can save time and energy in the triage process. If this is done correctly, the system tests will be much more likely to find code issues and not fail because of issues within the environment. If you are still seeing system tests fail because of non-code issues, you probably have holes in your post-deployment checks that should be plugged to help isolate environment/deployment issues and improve the triage process.

Continuous Delivery Implementation

The principles of CD are well designed to address the challenges faced by most traditional enterprise organizations deploying code across multiple servers. Determining where to start, though, can be a bit overwhelming for most large organizations, because this magnitude of change can take several months to years. Therefore, you need to start where the changes will have the most benefit.

It may be tempting to start "doing CD" by just taking one application and implementing all the CD approaches to learn everything about CD before

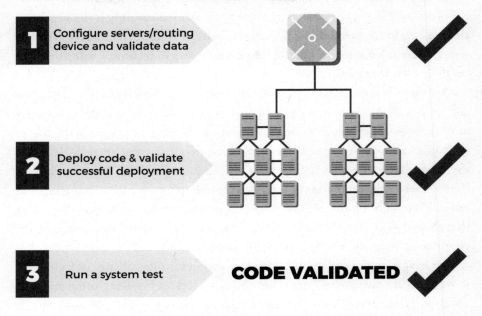

FIGURE 15B: FINDING THE OFFENDING COMPONENT QUICKLY IMPROVES PRODUCTIVITY

1 Configure servers/routing device and validate data

2 Deploy code & validate successful deployment

3 Run a system test   **CODE VALIDATED**

rolling it out broadly. This will work well if that component can be developed, qualified, and deployed independently. If instead you are working with a tightly coupled architecture, this approach is not going to work. It will take awhile to implement all those steps for one application, and since it still can't be deployed independently, it won't provide any benefits to the business. When this happens, your transformation is at risk of losing momentum because everyone knows you are investing in CD but they are not seeing or feeling any improvements in their day-to-day work.

This is why it is important to use the business objectives from chapter 6 to prioritize the implementation. Providing feedback to developers in an operation-like environment is a key first step that starts helping the organization right away. It forces the different teams to resolve the integration and production issues on a daily basis when they are cheaper and easier to fix. It also encourages the cultural change of having the organization prioritize coordinating the work across teams to deliver value to the customer instead of local optimizations in dedicated environments. It gets Development and Operation teams focused on the common objective of proving the code will work in a production-like environment, which starts to lower the cultural barrier between the two groups. You start ensuring the developers prioritize making sure their changes will work in production with all the other code instead of just writing new features. **Determining if the organization will embrace these cultural changes up front is important because if they won't, there is no sense in making big investments in technical solutions that on their own won't help**.

Once it is clear the organization will commit to the cultural changes, deploying and testing all the code in this production-like environment as many times a day as possible provides the additional advantage of helping to prioritize the rest of the technical improvements. By increasing the frequency, you are making visible the issues that have been plaguing your organization for years. This process helps clarify what is most important to standardize and speed up with automation. For example, to speed up the frequency it is important to start automating the things that change most, like code, so it usually makes sense to start with automating the continuous integration and deployment process.

The next steps depend on where you are seeing the most change or feeling the most pain. If your environments are changing lots and causing problems with consistency, then you know you need to implement scripted environments. If database changes are giving you problems, then you can prioritize the evolutionary database work. If keeping the test automation passing every day requires constantly updating or changing tests, then your framework needs to be rearchitected for maintainability. If your team is spending lots of time triaging between deployment and code issues, work on creating post-deployment tests. **The important point is to let the pain of increasing the frequency on this production-like environment drive the priority of your technical changes**. This will force you to fix the issues in priority order and provide the fastest time to value for the transformation.

Summary

Applying DevOps principles at scale for enterprise solutions delivered across servers is going to require implementing CD. This is a big effort for most large organizations. Because it requires cultural changes, you want to make sure this transition is as efficient as possible to avoid resistance to the changes that happen when it takes too long. Architecting the approach to efficiently leverage common code and knowing where to start is essential. The pipeline should be designed with an orchestrator that will enable leverage of common components and avoid the creation of monolithic scripts that are hard to maintain. Designing scripted environment and scripted deployment with common scripts that have an approach for separately describing the differences between environments will help get Development and Operations working toward common goals with common tools.

Once there is a good architecture design, the next most important step is determining which changes to take on in which order. These priorities should be based off the business objectives and where you will get the biggest return on your investment. Executives should also prioritize changes that start the cultural shifts that are required early before you invest too much time and energy in technical solutions. It should consider which components are changing most frequently and what is causing the most pain in the deployment process. Implementing CD in a large, traditional organization is going to take some time and effort, but it is worth the effort because it will require fixing issues that have been undermining the effectiveness of your organization for years.

CHAPTER 10

DESIGNING THE DEPLOYMENT PIPELINE

Providing quick feedback to developers and maintaining a more stable code base are essential to improving the productivity of software development in large, traditional organizations. Developers want to do a good job, and they assume they have until they get feedback to the contrary. If this feedback is delayed by weeks or months, then it can be seen as beating up developers for defects they don't even remember creating. If feedback comes within a few hours of the developer commit and the tools and tests can accurately identify which commits introduced the problem, the feedback gets to engineers while they are still thinking about and working on that part of the code.

This type of feedback actually helps the developers become better coders instead of just beating them up for creating defects. Even better, if it is very good feedback with an automated test that they can replicate on their desktop, then they can quickly identify the problem and verify the fix before recommitting the code. For large, traditional organizations with tightly coupled architectures, it is going to take time and effort to design the test stages of the deployment pipeline to appropriately build up a stable system.

Principles Driving the Design

Working to quickly localize the offending code down to the fewest number of developers possible is the basic principle that should drive design. This can be accomplished with two complimentary approaches.

First, more frequent build and test cycles means that fewer developers have committed code since the last build. Second, build up stable components or applications that get qualified and progressed forward to larger integrations of the enterprise system. Ideally the entire system would be fully deployed and tested with every new commit to quickly localize any system issues immediately down to an individual. This, though, is just not practical for most large, traditional organizations. Therefore, you need to design a deployment pipeline that moves as close to that ideal state as possible but accommodates the current realities of your traditional business.

Testing Layers

The first step in any testing process is unit testing and static code analysis to catch as many defects as quickly as possible. In fact, we can't think of any good reason why a developer would ever be allowed to check in code with broken unit tests. The advantage of unit tests is that if properly designed, they run very fast and can quickly localize any problems. The challenges with unit tests for lots of large, traditional organizations are twofold: First, due to their tightly coupled architectures, traditional organizations are not able to effectively find most of the defects with unit tests. Second, going back through lots of legacy code to add unit tests is seldom realistic until that part of the code is being updated.

The second step in the testing process to qualify code before final integration is component- or service layer-testing at clean interfaces. This should be used where possible because these tests run faster, and the interfaces should be more stable than the true user interface-based system testing.

The final step that can be very effective for finding the important integration issues in large, traditional organizations is user interface-based system testing. The challenge with these tests is that they typically run slowly and can require running the entire enterprise software system. Therefore you have to think carefully about when and where they are used.

Designing Test Stages

Ideally you would run every test on every check-in with every component that needs to work together. This is not practical for most large, traditional organizations that have tightly coupled architectures requiring long-running system tests and hundreds or thousands of developers working on software that must work together in production. Therefore, you need to design a test stage strategy that localizes the feedback to the smallest number of developers possible while finding as many of the integration and operational issues as possible.

This strategy is accomplished in three ways. First, build and test as much of the system as possible, as often as possible as one unit. Second, break down and simplify the problem by using service virtualization to isolate different parts of the system. Third, pick a subset of the testing for fast feedback before promoting the code forward to more stages for more extensive testing. This subset of tests defines the minimal level of stability that you will allow in the system at each stage of code progression. They go by different names in different organizations, but for the purpose of this example we will refer to them as build acceptance tests.

Where possible, the best solution is to build up and test the system as often as possible in an environment that is as close to production as it can be. While not always practical, it should be the first choice where possible. Localizing the issues to the smallest number of commits and developers by reducing the time window between test executions provides the advantage of finding as many of the system integration and operational issues as possible as early and as cheaply as possible. It can be challenging, though, to get everyone working together to keep the build green if it becomes too large or complex with different organizations providing code at different levels of stability. Additionally, if there are frequent build failures, it might be difficult to get someone to own the resolution of the issue. Therefore, in large organizations, it frequently makes sense to break the problem down into smaller, manageable pieces that can be built up into a larger, stable system.

Service virtualization is a very effective tool for helping to break up a very large enterprise system into manageable pieces. Isolating components from other parts of the system has the advantage of allowing you to localize the feedback to developers working on just one part of the enterprise system while simultaneously running system tests. Different teams can make progress independently creating new capabilities against a known interface with the service virtualization, then start end-to-end testing once both sides are ready. The disadvantages are creating virtualization that will have to be maintained and the potential for the virtualization to be different from the actual interface with the other component. Therefore, virtualization should be used as little as possible, but it is an important tool for building up testing stages for enterprise software systems.

For very large organizations, virtualization should be considered for interfaces across significant organizational boundaries to help localize the ownership of issues. It can also be a very helpful approach for working across teams using different development methodologies like Agile and Waterfall because it allows independence of development models while forcing cross-organizational alignment with working code. The different groups can work independently and make progress with the virtual service.

This works well as long as teams are removing the virtual service when the code is ready for true end-to-end testing, ideally daily, to ensure the actual enterprise system stays stable even though the teams are using different management approaches. Instead of forcing the convergence of all the development processes, start with integrating stable code on a more frequent basis. This will help align the Waterfall organization with the business value of having a more stable code base without forcing them to embrace Agile as a completely new development methodology. The beauty of doing it this way is that the Waterfall organizations will start evolving toward always-releasable code, which is one of the biggest advantages of Agile.

The next big step for them in applying Agile and DevOps principles at scale is just creating a prioritized backlog. Then, over time, if they choose to they can start implementing Agile process changes at the team level. This approach gets the entire organization moving toward the business benefits of Agile without requiring a "big bang" Agile transformation across the enterprise. **Can you see how this approach gets the Waterfall parts of the organization started on the journey towards the business benefits of Agile with less organizational turmoil than the classic approach we described in chapter 2?**

Figure 16 shows how this might work. In this case, each component should start with a build, making sure all the unit tests pass. The next step is to build and system test the Agile components on the left of the graphic with the rest of the Waterfall components running against the virtual service. You want to do this as many times a day as possible using your build acceptance tests. This enables finding the integration issues between the Agile components and most of the integration issues between the Agile and Waterfall components. We say *most* of the issues because the virtual service will not be a perfect substitution for the Waterfall components. An additional benefit is being able to isolate the Agile code progression from the periods of instability that originally exist in most Waterfall development processes. The Agile components are not held up for weeks or months while the Waterfall components are undergoing these periods of instability. It also optimizes the speed of feedback and localizes the feedback to a smaller number of developers by increasing the frequency of the build for the Agile components.

The most extensive set of automated testing should be run at this stage. The objective here is to be able to fully test the Agile components as a system so the issues can be isolated and fixed as a smaller component of the larger system. Then

FIGURE 16: BUILDING UP THE ENTERPRISE SYSTEM

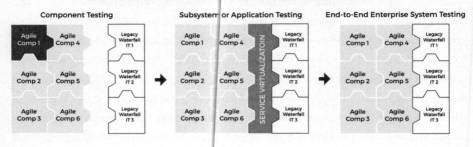

take a subset of the automated tests that will fully test the interface and have them run against the full enterprise system with the virtual service removed. Running a subset of tests that fully exercise this interface in the entire system, ideally on a daily basis, has the advantage of ensuring there are no disconnects between the virtual service and the actual code. The other advantage of this approach is that the majority of the full regression testing can be run on smaller, less expensive environments that only represent the Agile components. The more expensive and complex enterprise environment is only used for the subset of tests that are required to validate the interface. For example, there may be hundreds of automated tests required to validate the Agile components that have the same use case against the interface. In this case, run the hundreds against the virtual service and then pick one of them to be part of the enterprise system test. This saves money and reduces the complexity of managing end-to-end testing. This is a simple example, but it shows how you can use build frequency and service virtualization in combination to help break down and build up complex software systems to localize feedback while moving the organization to more stable system.

Defining the Build Acceptance Test

The third approach to designing the test stages is to break the long-running system tests into groups with different objectives. System testing has huge advantages for traditional organizations in quality of feedback to developers. The tradeoff is the timeliness of this feedback and how it is incorporated into code progression. Therefore, these system tests need to be broken into stages to optimize coverage while at the same time minimizing the delay in the feedback. While unit and component testing are the first priority, there also needs to be an effective strategy for system tests. There should be a clear subset of build acceptance system tests that are designed to get the best coverage as quickly as possible.

These build acceptance tests are probably the most valuable tool available because they are used to drive up the stability and quality of the code base. In traditional continuous integration systems, this is where you would turn the build red. The build acceptance tests define the absolute minimum level of stability that will ever be allowed in the code base. If these tests fail, then getting them fixed is the top priority for the entire Development organization and nobody is allowed to check in code until they are fixed. **This is a big cultural change for most organizations. It requires management reinforcing expected behaviors through extensive communication. It also requires the rest of the organization to hold off any check-ins until things get fixed, which slows down the entire organization. A more effective approach, as discussed before, is to use your systems to enforce the behaviors by automatically blocking code that does not pass the build acceptance tests from ever being committed to trunk in the source code management (SCM) tool.**

Building Up the Enterprise System

The next step is to combine gated commits and build acceptances tests with the process of building up and integrating a large enterprise software system in order to balance progressing code through the system quickly to find integration issues with keeping the code base stable. As discussed earlier, from a change management perspective it is best if you can have your system gate commitments at the SCM level in order to keep the code base stable and to provide feedback to a small group of developers. You don't want the offending code to ever make it into the repository. Ideally, you would want all your tests run against the entire enterprise system before letting code into the SCM to optimize stability. The problem with this approach is the length of time required for feedback to the developer and the time it takes to get code onto trunk and progress through the system.

The most pragmatic approach is to gate commitments into the SCM at the point in the deployment pipeline where you optimized for frequency of builds on subcomponents of the enterprise system. This automates keeping the trunk stable for components that have fast build and test cycles. After this point you can also gate the components building up into the enterprise system based on artifacts or applications, as depicted in figure 17.

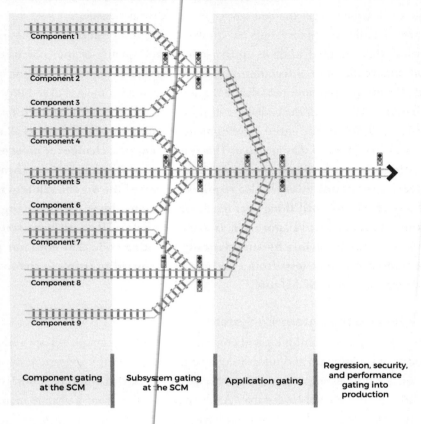

Component 1
Component 2
Component 3
Component 4
Component 5
Component 6
Component 7
Component 8
Component 9

Component gating at the SCM

Subsystem gating at the SCM

Application gating

Regression, security, and performance gating into production

This has the advantage of keeping the enterprise system stable while allowing components to quickly get code onto trunk. The disadvantage occurs when there is code that makes it through subsystem testing but breaks the enterprise-level system testing. The broken artifact creates a train wreck for this application by blocking new versions of the application from integrating into the enterprise system. The developers, however, can still keep developing and committing code to the SCM as long as they pass the application build acceptance tests. In this case, you need someone working to ensure the application is fixed and then letting the build process know this new version of the application is ready for another enterprise-level integration, as depicted in figure 18. This is a manual process and, therefore, you are at risk of nobody taking ownership of fixing the issue and having stale applications in the enterprise integration.

FIGURE 18: APPLICATION GATING

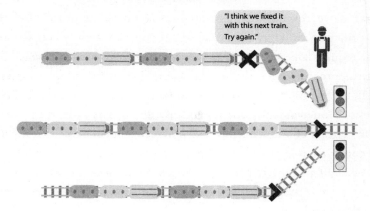

To avoid this, you are going to need a good process for providing visibility of the artifact aging to everyone in the organization. Figure 17 depicts using your deployment pipeline to build up stable components into a stable enterprise system. This supports the basic Agile principle of keeping the code base stable so it is economical to do more frequent smaller releases.

FIGURE 19: LOOSELY COUPLED ARCHITECTURE
DEPLOYMENT PIPELINE

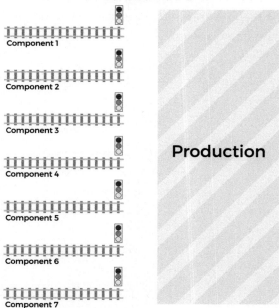

Architectural Implications on the Deployment Pipeline Complexity

In chapter 8 we covered architectural impact on the approach for applying DevOps principles in larger organizations. If you have tightly coupled architectures that require large groups of people working together, then you need very structured approaches, like the one in figure 17, to build up complex stable systems. If, on the other hand, you have loosely coupled architectures that enable small teams to independently develop, qualify, and release code, then you are able realize the benefits of a much simpler deployment pipeline like the one in figure 19. This comparison is provided to help encourage executives to ensure they are finding the right pragmatic balance between developing processes for building up complex, stable systems and making the architectural changes required to decouple the complexity.

Summary

Building up a stable enterprise system is a key component of the DevOps or Agile principle of enabling more frequent and smaller releases. Even if your business does not require or support more frequent releases, it helps with developer productivity and takes uncertainty out of the endgame. That said it is not a natural outcome of most enterprise Agile implementations that start with a focus on the team. Therefore, it is going to require focus from the leadership team to design and implement these improvements.

CHAPTER 11

IMPROVING STABILITY OVER TIME

Once the fundamentals are in place and you have started applying DevOps principles at scale, you are ready to start improving stability. The basics of starting this change management process were covered in chapter 7.

This chapter covers how to increase stability of the enterprise system using build acceptance tests and the deployment pipeline. This next step is important because the closer the main code base gets to production-level quality, the more economical it is to do more frequent, smaller releases and get feedback from customers. **Additionally, having a development process that integrates stable code across the enterprise is one of the most effective ways of aligning the work across the teams, which, as we have discussed before, is the first-order effect for improving productivity.**

Depending on the business, your customers may not require or even allow overly frequent releases, but keeping the code base more stable will help find integration issues early before there are large investments in code that won't work well together. It will also make your Development teams much more productive because they will be making changes to a stable and functioning code base.

Even if you are not going to release more frequently than you currently do, you will find keeping the code base more stable will help improve productivity. If your organization does want to move to continuous deployment, trunk (not branches) should be driven to production levels of stability, such that any new development can be easily released into production. Regardless of your need for CD, the process for improving stability on the trunk is going to be a big transformation that requires managing the automated tests and the deployment pipeline. In this chapter we will show how to improve stability over time.

Understanding the Work between Release Branch and Production

The first step in improving stability and enabling smaller, more frequent releases requires understanding the work that occurs between release branch and production. At this stage, development is ideally complete and you are going through the final stages of making sure the quality is ready for customers. For leading-edge companies doing CD, the trunk is always at production levels of stability and this only takes minutes. For most large, traditional organizations, though, this is a long and painful process, and getting better is going to take some time.

The first step in reducing the time and effort required between release branch and production is characterizing the work required in that phase of your development process.

The graph in figure 20 is a good representation of the work in the system to get the code base releasable. The exact specifics for your business may be different, but the idea of having all the information on one chart will be very valuable for understanding the characteristics of the project readiness so you can drive time and work out of the system. The bars track the daily status of completion for all the stories planned in the release. The dots at the bottom track the number of days a green build with the latest code has passed the build acceptance testing and was ready for automated regression testing. The graph also tracks the number of open defects and the automated test passing rates.

To get the code ready for release, all the stories need sign-off, the defects need to be fixed or deferred, and the test passing rates need to meet release criteria. Additionally, to accomplish all these things in a timely manner, the deployment pipeline needs to be delivering green builds with the latest code on a regular basis. You can see how when there is a red build on days 2, 4, and 7 the metrics go flat because when you can't process code through the deployment pipeline, you can't validate any of the code changes. You can also see that the time delay between release branch and production is driven by the time it takes to complete all the stories, fix all the defects, and get the tests passing. This one graphic allows you to quickly visualize all the work left in the system. The closer trunk is to release quality, the less work required for getting the release into production. Therefore, the goal is to improve the stability of trunk so there is less work overall.

The Role of Project Management

The first step, and technically the easiest in terms of improving stability of trunk at the time of release branch, is making stability an important part of the milestone criteria from a project-management perspective. If project management focuses the release-branching milestone on completing features, then that will be the focus of the organization. Everyone will be so busy getting features in at the last

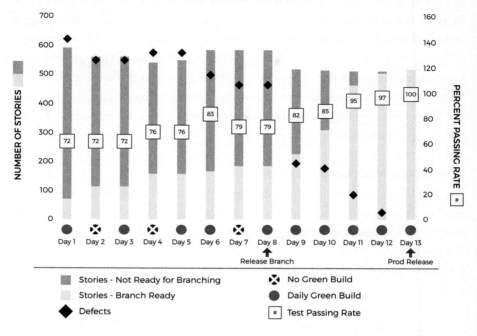

FIGURE 20: RELEASE READINESS

Legend:
- Stories - Not Ready for Branching
- Stories - Branch Ready
- Defects
- No Green Build
- Daily Green Build
- # Test Passing Rate

minute that stability will tend to take a hit. If instead the release branch requires all features to be signed off on, with no open defects and test automation at an acceptable level of coverage and passing rates, then there will be a more stable trunk and, therefore, less work in the end game.

If the organization has historically focused on features, it will take some time to adjust to this new way. Your project-management group will have to work to steadily increase these criteria over time. They must be willing to kick projects out of the release if they are not ready. A good example of the value of this is shown in figure 22, where kicking a small portion of stories out of the release on the branching day resulted in a big drop in defects and an increase in test passing on the day after. This last step is usually hard for traditional organizations because the business may want the new capability really badly. **The problem with this is that when the management team wants a new capability really badly, it tends to get it that way in terms of quality.**

Allowing new features that are not ready into a release tends to delay the release and impacts the productivity of all the other projects in the release. The key is helping the organization understand those tradeoffs and see the value of improving stability at release branch over time. **If executives can't drive these cultural shifts in the release process, then they shouldn't bother investing in technical solutions like CD because they won't work.** This is another example of why we say the capacity of the organization to handle change is your most precious resource and the cultural changes are the most challenging. The executives are going to need to focus their change management capacity in places like this where it will improve the process the most, which won't work if they are asking for too many changes all at once.

Statistically Managing Test Results

The next biggest opportunity for reducing the amount of work after release branch involves driving up the stability of trunk with automated testing. This ensures that everything is stable and that there are not a lot of open defects in the system. It is a pretty big step for most traditional enterprise organizations, so it is going to take some time and effort. It is also going to require a very structured approach.

Previously, we covered how to design tests that are maintainable and can

FIGURE 21: FARMING THE BUILD ACCEPTANCE

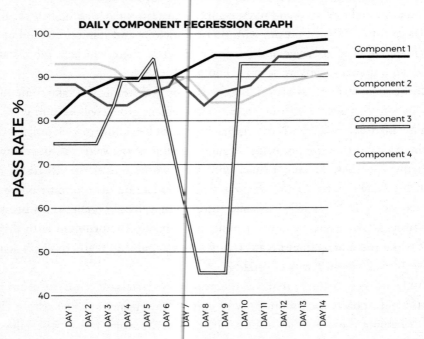

quickly localize failure to the right component. We have also talked about how to break tests into different stages and the role of build acceptance tests for defining the minimal acceptable level of quality. Now we are going to cover how to bring it all together to improve the stability of trunk. If you have the proper test automation framework, use techniques like Page Object Models, and then write tests that localize failures to the offending component, you can start statistically managing your test results. Figure 21 illustrates how powerful this combination of tools and processes can be.

Note in the graph that our regression suite is broken up into a set of component test suites. For the past several days, each of the component test suites has been running, and each has a pass rate of 75–95%. However, on day 8 when we arrive at work, we see that the component 4 test suite has a passing rate of only 45%. Even though the tests are being run on a fully-integrated system, each component test suite only exercises the functionality associated with its component, so we now know that something happened to the code for that component. Since we run our entire regression suite every day, we have another very powerful piece of information. Because these same tests were passing at >90% on day 6 and they are passing at 45% on day 8, we know that the offending code was checked in sometime between those two test runs. Because we have our code under strict SCM control, it is easy to see who checked in code for this component. You know the short list of developers who checked in code, you know when it was checked in, and you know exactly what functionality was broken.

Compared to an organization that did not invest in a solid foundation including a robust automation framework, component-based testing, etc., the organization that did make these investments is light-years ahead and the productivity gains are dramatic. We've seen many organizations that have pursued both paths, and we've pursued both ourselves. In all cases, the ROI on this investment is substantial. You simply will never achieve the full benefit of Agile development until you get your automated testing properly built out and integrated into the development pipeline.

Farming Your Build Acceptance Tests to Increase Trunk Stability

This example illustrates another important capability. When you see a component test suite take a dramatic pass-rate drop like this, you need to ask yourself, "How did code that broke that many tests make its way into my repository?" A developer who has rebased their environment since this code came in is now working on a system that is fundamentally broken, and this will impact their productivity until the issue is resolved. This is especially true of the team that owns this functionality. Other developers on this team will continue to work on other tasks and their work will be tested by these same tests. Because these tests are already failing at a high rate, the developers have no way to know if their code has introduced a new set of issues. Essentially, you've allowed the train wreck to happen directly on your development trunk because your gating did not protect you.

The good news is that this problem is easy to solve. You have some set of build acceptance tests that are gating the code check-ins, but they allowed this problem to make its way into the code base. You've got a large number of tests in your component test suite that readily detected the problem. All you need to do is identify the best candidate tests and promote them into the build acceptance test suite. The next time a similar problem occurs, the build acceptance tests will likely detect it and cause the offending code to be rejected and sent back to the developer.

While finding the issue within 24 hours of when it was introduced and getting that information to a small group of developers who committed code is good, getting the same information to an even smaller group within a few hours of the commit is even better. This is why we strongly suggest that you actively manage which tests are in the build acceptance test suite to ensure you have the most effective tests in place to gate the check-in. Harvesting tests from your regression suite is a great way to help keep the build acceptance tests fresh and relevant.

This same approach can also be used to drive passing rates up over time. If your overall component tests are passing at 85%, can you find a defect fix that will drive that up to 90%? If so, get that defect fixed and then add a test to the build acceptance test suite to ensure those tests keep passing. You can continue this process of farming your build acceptance tests over time to drive up the stability of trunk. If you are a website or SaaS that is driving for CD, this requires driving trunk to production levels of stability. If your business model does not support that frequency of release, there are still real benefits to driving up the stability of trunk, but you might start getting diminishing returns for a very large number of tests needing to pass at over 90% every day.

At HP we had ~15,000 computer hours of tests running every day on trunk. We found that driving the passing rates to around 90% was very valuable, even though we were just doing quarterly releases. On the other hand, we found that driving the passing rates up to 98% required a lot of extra effort that slowed down our throughput and did not provide much additional benefit. Therefore, if your business requires less frequent releases it is going to be important to find the right balance between stability and throughput.

Embedded Firmware Example

The concepts for designing the test stages and building up the enterprise system work equally well for embedded, packaged, and web/cloud solutions. There are, however, some unique considerations for embedded software and firmware. This is because while in addition to building up the components and progressing through stages of testing, you also have to consider moving through different test environments to build up to more operational-like product environments.

Depending on the availability of the final product and emulators, you might have to rely extensively on simulators for gating all the code into the SCM. If your embedded solution is broken into components that are more software-like versus embedded firmware interacting with custom ASICs, then you should work to gate the software components with simulators and save the emulator gates for the lower-level firmware. Additionally, give consideration to the build acceptance tests at the simulator, emulator, and product level, which may be different given the objectives of each stage. Either way, you should not wait too long before ensuring the build stays at an acceptable level of stability for every test environment leading up to and including the final product.

In the LaserJet example, we used some but not all of these principles. In figure 22, you can see the different stages of testing from L1 through L4. L1 we optimized for frequency of build and used as the gate for getting into the SCM. Additionally, we broke it down into stage 1 and stage 2 to stop simple mistakes at the individual level before progressing the code into an integrated build with 10–30 developers. This tended to slow down the time required to get code into the SCM, but it drove up the pass rates for the stage 2 builds. In this case the developers found they preferred to wait up to four hours for a build that was likely to pass than to have to recommit because they were in a build with someone else that had a significant problem. The code base was ~10M line of code with 400-plus developers committing code over 100 times per day. With this size of a continuous integration system in a traditional organization, we found optimizing

FIGURE 22: CONTINUOUS INTEGRATION AND TEST SYSTEM

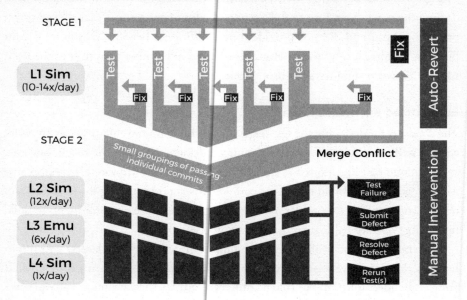

for stability over speed provided the best breakthroughs in productivity, which is contrary to what some consultants would recommend.

We designed the next stages of testing to localize the offending code that would break different stages of testing using the componentization approach. The quality bar was a fairly small subset of testing that defined the minimal level of acceptable stability. L2 got into more extensive testing spread across a couple dozen simulators and ran every two hours. The intent of this stage was to provide much better code coverage on a slightly less frequent basis. Each L2 build included a few L1 builds. In this case we were looking for commits that broke a significant percentage of L2 tests that were not caught by L1. L3 ran every four hours on emulators to catch interactions with the hardware. Then L4 was a full regression test that was run every day on the simulators. In addition, while not shown on this graphic, we ran basic acceptance testing every day on the final products under development.

This example shows that we worked to optimize the amount of testing and defects we were able to find using simulators and emulators. Since we had over 15,000 hours of automated testing to run each day, it would have been impossible to run them all on real printers. It is impractical to get that many printers and you would have to print millions of pages a day on real paper. It would have cost too much, and there are not enough trees in Idaho to make enough paper to run all that testing without simulator and emulators. Therefore, we needed a strategy to minimize the costs of running these tests to provide feedback to developers affordably. As we moved from simulators to emulators to the final product we got closer to the final production environment, but the cost of testing also went up significantly. To combat this, we ran our most frequent automated testing on simulators but then validated subsets on emulators and the final products. Then, every time we found a defect that did not show up on the simulator or emulator, we worked hard to enhance the capabilities of those tools so we could catch it upstream next time.

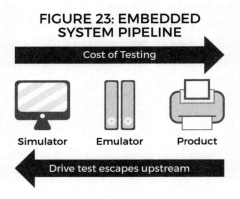

FIGURE 23: EMBEDDED SYSTEM PIPELINE

We know lots of organizations are still developing embedded software and firmware on simulators and emulators that they don't trust to find defects. They have found over time that these tools are just missing too many real defects, but they have not taken the time to invest in improving their tools. If you are going to transform the development processes of a large embedded group, the first step needs to be ensuring you have simulators and emulators you can trust for finding defects and a team to improve them over time.

Summary

Applying DevOps principles at scale really requires the executive to drive the cultural and technical changes for improving the stability of trunk. This is vitally important because of the productivity gains that are possible when you eliminate branches and integrate all work across the teams on trunk. To get your code trunk to this level of quality and to keep it there, you need to begin using a CD pipeline with both code and component-level gating. This pipeline must incorporate a robust test automation framework. You will need to have component-based automated tests. Executives will need some simple metrics that are auto-generated each day to understand what is working and what is not so that they can focus resources in the right place every day.

To be fair, building systems of this type that include a robust automation framework is not easy and not to be undertaken by the faint of heart. It takes software engineers of the highest quality to design, implement, and maintain such a pipeline and framework. Coupled with well-written component tests, however, the payoff is substantial. You can now have multiple component test sets running each day, and by watching the trend line of each, you can quickly determine which parts of your system are working and which are not. With this information, you can get your teams focused on the quality of each component and apply the right resources at the right time to start changing the process and culture.

ꟾꟾꟾꟾꟾ CHAPTER 12
GETTING STARTED

Executives need to make sure they don't let the magnitude of the overall change keep them from starting on improving the processes. We understand that taking on this big of a change in a large organization can be a bit overwhelming, which might cause some executives to question leading the effort. They need to understand that while leading the transformation is a big challenge, trying to compete in the market with traditional software development processes is going to be even more challenging as companies around them improve.

Instead of worrying about the size of the challenge or how long it is going to take, executives just need to make sure they start the enterprise-level continuous improvement process. There is really no bad software development process. There is only how you are doing it today and better.

The key is starting the process of continually improving. The first step is making sure you have a clear set of business objectives that you can use to prioritize your improvements and show progress along the journey. Next is forming the team that will lead the continuous improvement process. The team should include the right leaders across Development, QA, Operations, and the business that will need to help support the priorities and lead the transformation. You need to help them understand the importance of this transformation and get them to engage in the improvement process.

As much as possible, if you can get these key leaders to help define the plan so they take ownership of its success, it is going to help avoid resistance from these groups over time. Nobody is going to know all the right answers up front, so the key is going to be moving through the learning and adjusting processes as a group.

The First Iteration

It is going to take a few months to get good at setting achievable monthly objectives and to ensure you are working on the right stuff. Don't let that slow you down. It is more important to get the process of continuous improvement and learning started than it is to get it perfectly right. After all, the worst that could happen is that you are wrong for a month before you have a chance to learn and adjust.

These objectives should include all the major objectives the organization has for the month, because if you have a separate set of priorities for the business deliverables and the improvement process, people are going to be confused about overall priorities. Therefore, make sure you have a one-page set of priorities that everyone agrees are critical to sustaining the business and improving the development processes.

The key deliverables for the business are going to be easy to define. Where to start the process changes may be a bit more unfamiliar for the team. We suggest you consider starting the process of improving the day-to-day stability of trunk. Set up a continuous integration process with some automated tests and start the process of learning to keep the builds green. If you are already doing this at the component level with unit tests, consider moving this to larger application builds in an operational-like environment with automated system tests. This starts the cultural change of getting all the different development groups getting all the code working together and out to the customer instead of working on some intermediate step. It also is a good opportunity to stress your test automation to ensure it is stable and maintainable. If it isn't, your developers will let you know right away. It is important to figure this out before you end up with a lot of automation you may need to throw away.

Make sure when you set the goals for the first month that they are quantifiable. Can you measure clearly whether the objective was met? Also make sure the organization feels the goals are important and achievable. This may take a little time to get the broader support, but it is important that people felt like the goal was doable up front. That way, when you later review why it wasn't accomplished, you can get people to clarify what is getting in the way of their ability to get things done. If it was a goal they never thought was possible, when it was not done they will say just that and there is nothing to learn. If instead they really felt it was possible and important, you are more likely to get an insightful response to what is impeding progress in your organization.

This is where the key learning and improvements really start to occur. The leadership team needs to take on the challenge of becoming investigative reporters spending time out in the organization learning what is working and what needs to be improved. They then need to take this new understanding to prioritize removing impediments for the organization. **It is this process of engaging with the organization to continually improve that will become your long-term competitive advantage.**

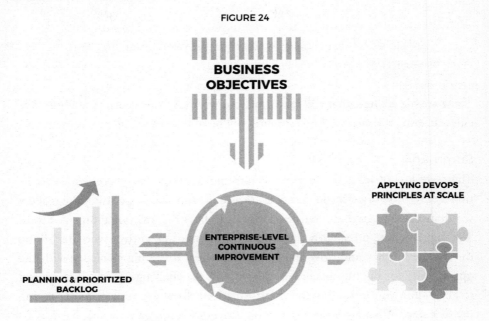

FIGURE 24

Leading the Key Cultural Changes

Executives need to understand that other than engaging with the organization in the continuous improvement process, their most important role is leading the cultural shifts for the organization. They will need to be involved and helping to prioritize the technical improvements but they need to understand that these investments will be a waste of time if they can't get the organization to embrace the following cultural shifts:

» Getting developers to own ensuring every check-in to trunk is stable in a production-like environment as job #1

» Getting Development and Operation teams using common tools and environments to align them on a common objective

» Getting the entire organization to agree that the definition of done at the release branch is that the feature is signed off, defects-free, and the test automation is ready in term of test coverage and passing rates

» Getting the organization to embrace the unique characteristics of software and design a planning process that takes advantage of its flexibility

These are big changes that will take time, but without the executives driving these cultural shifts the technical investments will be of limited value.

Summary

There are lots of ideas for improving software development processes for traditional enterprise organizations. There are also documented case studies that show the dramatic impact these transformations can have on traditional organizations. The biggest thing missing in the industry is engaged executives who are willing to lead the journey and drive the cultural changes. It is a big challenge with the opportunity for big improvements. Are you up the challenge? Who do you need to get to join you in leading the transformation? What are your plans for taking the first step? What are your business objectives? What organizational barriers do you think you will need to address? What do you think your organization can commit to completing in the first iteration of your enterprise-level continuous improvement process? What are you waiting for? Let's get the journey started!

FURTHER READING

Lean Enterprise: How High Performance Organizations Innovate at Scale
Jez Humble, Joanne Molesky, and Barry O'Reilly

This is the most important book executives should be reading as soon as they have developed the ability to release on a more frequent basis. It shows how to take advantage of this new capability to address the 50% of features that are never used or do not meet their intended business objectives.

A Practical Approach to Large-Scale Agile Development
Gary Gruver, Mike Young, and Pat Fulghum

This is a good, easy-to-read case study that will give the reader a good feel for the transformation journey of one organization. It provides more details on the HP experience referenced heavily in this book.

Toyota Kata: Managing People for Improvement, Adaptiveness, and Superior Results
Mike Rother

This book provides a manufacturing example of how a continuous improvement culture can be a long-term competitive advantage. There are a lot of similarities to what is being done in software, but readers should be aware that software processes are also different from manufacturing. Work is unique each time instead of being repetitive, so it is going to more difficult to get a quantitative feel for each change. Software leaders are going to have to spend time in the organization getting a more qualitative feel for the effect of the change.

Cucumber & Cheese: A Tester's Workshop
Jeff Morgan

This book should be read by lead developers and lead testers to ensure you are creating an automated testing framework that is maintainable and that quickly localizes defects.

Continuous Delivery: Reliable Software Releases through Build, Test, and Deployment Automation
Jez Humble and David Farley

This is a must-read for all your engineers working on Continuous Delivery.

Refactoring Databases: Evolutionary Database Design
Scott W. Ambler and Pramod J. Sadalage

This is must-read for all your database administrators and anyone telling you that trunk can't be always releasable due to database schema changes.

ACKNOWLEDGMENTS

Many people have contributed to this book. We would like to thank everyone we have worked with over the years that helped us better understand how to develop software. The ideas shared in this book are an accumulation of everything we have learned from working with each of you on a constant journey of improving software development processes. Without these discussions and debates, our understanding would not be as rich and the book would not be as complete.

We would like to thank everyone that has taken time to give us feedback on early versions of the book (in alphabetical order): Arun Dutta, Jim Highsmith, Jez Humble, Vinod Peris, Mary Poppendieck, Tom Poppendieck, and Lance Sleeper. Your input significantly improved the final product.

We would also like to thank the production staff at IT Revolution: Kate Sage, Robyn Crummer-Olson, Todd Sattersten, and Gene Kim. Your rigor and approach forced clarity of thought and crispness of message. We thank you, and our readers will benefit from a shorter and easier-to-read book.